Bridging

Bridging

A Teacher's Guide
to Metaphorical Thinking

Sharon L. Pugh
Indiana University

Jean Wolph Hicks
University of Louisville

Marcia Davis
Indiana University

Tonya Venstra
Indiana University

National Council of Teachers of English
1111 Kenyon Road, Urbana, Illinois 61801

ERIC Clearinghouse on Reading and Communication Skills
Indiana University, Smith Research Center, Suite 150
2805 East Tenth Street, Bloomington, Indiana 47408-2698

Permissions acknowledgments appear on page 150.

Manuscript Editor: Jane M. Curran

Production Editor: Rona S. Smith

Cover Design: Victoria Martin Pohlmann

Interior Design: Doug Burnett

NCTE Stock Number 03847-3050

Published 1992 by the National Council of Teachers of English, 1111 Kenyon Road, Urbana, Illinois 61801, and the ERIC Clearinghouse on Reading and Communication Skills, Indiana University, Smith Research Center, Suite 150, 2805 East Tenth Street, Bloomington, Indiana 47408-2698.

It is the policy of NCTE in its journals and other publications to provide a forum for the open discussion of ideas concerning the content and the teaching of English and the language arts. Publicity accorded to any particular point of view does not imply endorsement by the Executive Committee, the Board of Directors, or the membership at large, except in announcements of policy, where such endorsement is clearly specified.

This publication was prepared with partial funding from the Office of Educational Research and Improvement, U.S. Department of Education, under contract no. RI88062001. Contractors undertaking such projects under government sponsorship are encouraged to express freely their judgment in professional and technical matters. Points of view or opinions, however, do not necessarily represent the official view or opinions of the Office of Educational Research and Improvement.

Library of Congress Cataloging-in-Publication Data

Bridging : a teacher's guide to metaphorical thinking / Sharon
    L. Pugh . . . [et al.].
        p.   cm.
    Includes bibliographical references (p.).
    ISBN 0-8141-0384-7
    1. Metaphor—Study and teaching.   2. Language and languages—Study and teaching.   3. Thought and thinking.   I. Pugh, Sharon L.
P301.5.M48B75   1992
418'.0071'2—dc20   91-39841
                                                          CIP

Contents

Introduction

In choosing the title for this book, we deliberately selected one of the most pervasive metaphors in the English language, the idea of "bridge." To name just a few of its associations, a bridge can imply passage, connection, cohesion, branching, support, strengthening, opportunity, and freedom. It can also imply vulnerability, destructibility, and danger. The ambiguity of the basic metaphor, perhaps, is what keeps it alive after many centuries of linguistic service. It is what makes it an effective metaphor for learning, which is an adventure with its attendant risks.

Bridges unite separate individuals and groups, but they may also be passageways of intrusion and attack. They allow us to venture out into the world, but they may lure us too far. Since they are physical structures, usually built by humans, they become functional only after a lot of work and expense, and then they are subject to human error. Bridges may be burned, too, and then we may find ourselves stranded.

The image of a bridge, however, is predominantly a positive one. In this book a bridge, or as we prefer to say, "bridging," connotes discovery, progress, enlightenment, and the expansion of understanding and experience, not to mention novelty, delight, and change. For us, bridging is a metaphor for striking out beyond the confines of any given state of knowledge into the new territory beyond. We believe that learning is an adventure in which the gains far surpass the risks.

As teachers of English, we had another reason for liking the metaphor "bridge." It is an Anglo-Saxon word with a venerable history reaching back through Middle and Old English into the Germanic protolanguages, where, Eric Partridge informs us, it originally meant "brow," that section of our faces that spans our noses and connects our eyes (1959). So *bridge* is itself a metaphor based on a part of the human form; thus, as George Lakoff and Mark Johnson have put it, "bridge" is a metaphor we live by, one of those so fundamentally embedded in our physical experience that it is probably a cognitive universal across human cultures (1980).

In this book we hope to build a solid and useful bridge between theory and practice. We have concentrated on providing material and ideas for bringing metaphorical thinking into the classroom in the context of language discussions. We intend our account to be interesting without being too technical. We are more concerned with the dynamics of metaphorical thinking than with its mechanisms, and we believe that most teachers who savor the richness and surprise of the English language will want to share the wealth with their students. Our book, therefore, is not a definitive account of our subject for scholars, but a heuristic foray into the wit, art, and genius of the language through which we think about our world and know it.

We have organized the book to link the conceptual with the concrete. Teaching ideas are integrated with discussions concerning the various roles that metaphorical thinking plays in human understanding and communications. Part I is about the nature of metaphors, here construed broadly to include all kinds of imaginative comparisons, and about what we mean by the term *metaphorical thinking*. Part II concerns the personal and cultural aspects of metaphors—their affective side—showing how they are deeply embedded in our sense of who we are as individuals and as groups. In Part III we address critical aspects of metaphorical thinking and the need to be aware of how metaphors can both illuminate and obscure our concepts of reality. In Part IV we turn teachers' attention to their own uses of metaphors, providing ideas for using this powerful tool in the classroom. We conclude with a request directed at our readers.

You can best judge the level and interest of your own students and can select and modify the activities accordingly. The lessons are set up to help teachers introduce students to new aspects of metaphorical thinking and writing, or to expand what they already know. You can pick and choose the resource materials to use with your students and for your own study of metaphorical thought.

Sharon L. Pugh
Jean Wolph Hicks
Marcia Davis
Tonya Venstra

I The Nature of Metaphors and Metaphorical Thinking

Metaphorical Thinking

But the greatest thing by far is to be a master of the metaphor. It is the only thing that cannot be learned from others; and it is also a sign of genius because a good metaphor implies an intuitive perception of the similarity in the dissimilar.

Aristotle, *Poetics*

As educators, we have as rich a vocabulary for varieties of thinking as Inuits and skiers have for kinds of snow, and for much the same reason. We articulate concepts that correspond with realities that are vital to us; thereby we achieve some precision in both communications and actions. Thus, we find it useful to speak of critical and creative thinking, analytical and holistic thinking, convergent and divergent thinking, and so on, not as if we could actually divide human thought into these categories, but in order to have concepts for discussing the activity of the mind and trying to guide its development. In this book we focus on the concept of metaphorical thinking, by which we mean, broadly, drawing parallels between apparently unrelated phenomena to gain insight, make discoveries, offer hypotheses, wage arguments, and accomplish other such useful purposes.

George Lakoff and Mark Johnson argue that "our ordinary conceptual system, in terms of which we both think and act, is fundamentally metaphorical in nature. . . . [T]he way we think, what we experience, and what we do every day is very much a matter of metaphor" (1980, 3). If we do not always realize that a word or phrase is a metaphor, it may be because it is a cliché, itself a metaphor based on the printer's term for ready-made blocks of type for frequently used phrases. Other metaphors have become almost too large to see, like those that have shaped cultural consciousness and even altered the course of human history. When Thoreau wrote, "If a man does not keep pace with his companions, perhaps it is because he hears a different drummer" (1948, 272), he figuratively defined our national creed of individualism. In one phrase, "iron curtain," Winston Churchill metaphorically created the Western world's political mindset for most of the second half of the twentieth century.

As children, we meet metaphors as riddles. Oedipus saved the city of Thebes by recognizing the metaphors in the Sphinx's riddle: What walks on four legs in the morning, two legs at noon, and three legs in the evening? Metaphors underlie our most traditional forms of stories: allegories, fables, and parables. One of the most famous metaphorical stories in Western culture is Plato's "Allegory of the Cave," in which common understanding is compared to the shadows of a cave, cast by a light that represents the enlightenment toward which we might strive.

Language, which Emerson described as "fossil poetry," comprises strata of metaphors that have been embedded over time, so that virtually everything we say has a metaphorical record. Lewis Thomas extends the metaphor of fossilization as evidence of the living nature of language. "Language grows and evolves," he writes, "leaving fossils behind." He goes on to develop this notion as follows:

> The individual words are like different species of animals. Mutations occur. Words fuse, and then mate. Hybrid words and wild varieties of compound words are progeny. Some mixed words are dominated by one parent while the other is recessive. The way a word is used this year is its phenotype, but it has a deeply seated, immutable meaning, often hidden, which is the genotype. (1974, 158)

The Native American writer Leslie Silko expresses this idea of deep meaning in language through the words of an old medicine man who stated that "the world is fragile":

> The word he chose to express "fragile" was filled with the intricacies of a continuing process, and with a strength inherent in spider webs across paths through sand hills where early in the morning the sun becomes entangled in each filament of web. It took a long time to explain the fragility and intricacy because no word exists alone, and the reason for choosing each word had to be explained with a story about why it must be said this certain way. (1986, 35)

Through metaphorical thinking, divergent meanings become unified into the underlying patterns that constitute our conceptual understanding of reality. Indeed, metaphor is so much a part of our thinking and learning processes that we usually do not think about the essential role it plays.

Technically speaking, a metaphor (from the Greek *metapherein*: "to bear change") is the transfer of a term from one object to another on the basis of a perceived similarity. It is not a simple transfer, however, but one that works both ways. For example, we might speak of an "embryonic idea," meaning one that has just "germinated," but that must go through a "gestation" period to become a "mature" concept. Here we have a chain of related metaphors in which we can see that two kinds of transfer occur.

The second object (an idea) receives a new connotation, that of an organic entity undergoing biological processes. But the terms (*embryonic*, *germinate*, *gestation*, and *mature*) also receive new meanings. Therefore we can see that metaphor involves not only *change*, but also *exchange*. Both meaning and language have been expanded in a way that is both logical and imaginative.

Consider, for example, the metaphorical impact of technology, of which the computer is a prime example. Representing a new form of literacy, computer technology borrows heavily from its predecessor, print technology, with such terms as *scratch pad*, *spread sheet*, and *scroll*. To acquire the new literacy, we have to expand and alter the meanings of terms that come from the old. Using concepts and terms from what we already know, of course, makes good sense for understanding the unfamiliar, and this is perhaps the most common way that metaphors are used.

In a similar way, we have metaphorically adapted terms associated with disease to describe computer malfunctions. This idea also is not new. We have long spoken of machines as "sick" and "dying." But we have never before had such an elaborate medical vocabulary as we now apply to computers with their viruses and their prescription programs, such as Virus Rx, Vaccine, Flu Shot, and AntiBody. This unprecedented willingness to share our organic status with a machine may signal a new kind of relationship between people and their inventions, illuminated by our metaphorical thinking and the lengths to which we are willing to carry it.

Thinking metaphorically, then, combines rational and intuitive processes in a way that is sophisticated and playful at the same time. Another computer example provides a good illustration of this aspect. Don Nilsen (1984) cites the use of the term "moby" (referring to the great white whale) to describe a huge database. Accordingly, the University of California library database is called "Melvil," referring to both Herman Melville, author of *Moby Dick*, and Melvil Dewey, author of the Dewey decimal classification. Such nomenclature is more than a clever name. It reflects the way in which metaphors enable us to attach the new to the known, to expand language, to demystify technology, and to have fun, all at the same time.

Metaphorical thinking, in summary, entails attending to likenesses, to relationships, and to structural features in seeking what Aristotle called "similarities in dissimilarities." It involves identifying conceptual categories that may not be obvious or previously acknowledged. Metaphorical thinking cuts across subject and discipline boundaries by making knowledge in one domain a guide for comprehending knowledge in another, with some transfer of meaning taking place in both directions. Comparison is at the heart of it, and the basic meaning of the term *transfer* also implies the idea of a bridge. To be a metaphorical thinker is to be a constructive learner, one who actively builds bridges from the known to the new.

Trying It Out

Experiencing Metaphorical Thinking

Before we can use metaphors deftly, we must become acquainted with our own metaphorical thinking. This lesson is intended to help students (and teachers) begin the task.

Finding novel and apt comparisons may seem simplistic until we begin to examine the complexities actually involved. When, however, we consider Sandburg's comparison of "fog" with "cat" in his famous poem, we realize that our own perceptions of cats and fog mold our structuring of the comparison and determine whether it works for us the way it did for the poet. Even for people who care little for cats and less for fog, the poet's perception of quietness in both speaks to the reader's understanding.

Comparisons are conceptual in nature and metaphorical in definition. One cannot define anything in terms of something else without viewing the comparison from one's own personal perspective. In this sense, metaphors are personal expressions, and the coining of metaphors is a revelation not only of the "similarity in dissimilarities" that Aristotle emphasized, but also of one's own thought and perceptions.

With this point in mind, the following lesson is intended to help students both experience the formation of metaphors and become introspective about the process involved in that formation. Finally, through discussion, students can form a clear idea of the elements essential to the formation of a perception that leads to a metaphor.

Activity 1

The following lesson incorporates different teaching strategies, including directive instruction, in which the teacher conveys information to students, and mediative instruction, in which the teacher guides students to individual insights and understandings. Background information is provided to prepare teachers for direct explanation. Use this information as appropriate for your classes, perhaps selecting, elaborating, and adapting the concepts.

Collect a box of familiar items, such as a cup, an apple, a light bulb, a candle, a sock, a hammer, a washrag, a hair curler, a pipe, a paper clip, a pencil, some postage stamps, a pack of cards—anything. Have at least as many items in the box as there are students in the class. Throughout the time you are working with this box, continue to add interesting items to it and encourage students to contribute items, too.

Select an object for which you have a clear conceptual comparison. For example, a light bulb is often a comparison for a bright idea. A candle flame is often a comparison for life. Start with a common, easily recognized metaphorical comparison.

Hold up the object for the class to view, state the comparison, and ask how many students have heard of the comparison. Make a list on the board of the qualities shared by the object and the concept. For example, a comparison between the mind and a sponge might be developed as follows:

Mind/brain	Sponge
Absorbs knowledge	Absorbs liquid
Holds knowledge	Holds liquid
Can be washed	Can be rinsed
Dries up when not used	Dries up when not used

Variations on this core lesson follow.

Activity 2   Display the contents of your box of common objects on a table. Give students a single concept, such as *knowledge*, and have them choose an object with which to form a metaphor for that concept. For example, a student might decide that knowledge is a pair of scissors because it can cut through confusion. The context for this metaphor would be the student's knowledge of how scissors work. The salient feature would be the common idea of cutting edges; the relationships might be the progressive cutting action and the notion of individual control of this action. The connection would be in the physical feel of a pair of scissors in the hand, comparable to the feel of having the right knowledge with which to address a problem. By identifying these components of their simple metaphors, students can develop their sense of the basic functioning of metaphors.

Activity 3   Using the same assortment of objects, give students several concepts and let them choose both the concepts and objects with which they will work. This lesson may be enhanced by having students work in small groups.

Activity 4   With the assortment of items back in the box, bring in a container with slips of paper containing many abstract concepts to be defined through metaphor. These could be written in the form of an incomplete metaphor, such as the following:

War is a _____.

Happiness is a _____.

Love is a _____.

Time is a _____.

An idea is a _____.

Health is a _____.

An argument is a _____.

Understanding is a _____

Learning is a _____.

Control is a _____.

Write each concept on two or three slips of paper, with enough slips for all students in the class. Then follow these procedures:

1. Students choose (sight unseen) one item from the box and one slip of paper from the container.

2. Students list the ways in which the concept is like the item from the box.

3. Students next list the ways in which the concept is not like the item from the box.

4. Students form groups with other students who have drawn the same concept; they share their lists and decide which comparisons they like best.

5. Groups share their metaphors with the class.

6. Write some of the original lists on the board so that the class can discuss the idea that metaphors—no matter how well constructed—are always partial comparisons. Metaphors are effective not because they bring out exact correspondences, but because they highlight certain elements that two items have in common.

7. Students discuss what they needed to know in order to formulate their metaphors, while someone lists their ideas on the board.

8. Students talk about the overall structure of the metaphor—its "holistic" sense—and the particular correspondences within it. For example, a pair of scissors is like the concept of *control* in that it is a tool you hold in your hand,which is the overall comparison. Like scissors, control might be said to have cutting edges, guiding power, and the possibility of either creative or destructive uses, which are correspondences within the metaphor.

9. Students can then consider popular or famous metaphors, such as "life is a beach" and "parting is such sweet sorrow," to see how these metaphors can be explained and whether the students find them meaningful.

Activity 5   Students bring their own objects to class to use in writing original metaphors explaining concepts of their own choosing. They discuss how each component of the metaphor relates to the other components. They might describe the dissimilarities also. Encourage the use of original metaphors in all forms of oral and written communication.

How Metaphors Work

Metaphors are not merely things to be seen beyond. In fact, one can see beyond them only by using other metaphors. It is as though the ability to comprehend experience through metaphor were a sense, like seeing or touching or hearing, with metaphors providing the only ways to perceive and experience much of the world. Metaphor is as much a part of our functioning as our sense of touch, and as precious.

George Lakoff and Mark Johnson, *Metaphors We Live By*

If someone says that misplaced items are like wandering cats and eventually will turn up again, how do we know what that means? To understand and appreciate the metaphor, we have to (1) know about cats and lost items, (2) perceive some structural likenesses between them, (3) identify significant correspondences between these structures, and (4) pick up the connotation of giving in to fate: we cannot do much to control the appearances or disappearances of either misplaced items or roving cats. To explain this process, Lakoff and Johnson (1980) have identified four elements in conceptual thinking that define the dynamics of metaphor:

1. Metaphors are *grounded*. We have to have some experience, whether direct or vicarious, with both the concept and the compared object. This familiarity, including sensory, emotional, and attitudinal experiences, will affect our understanding of the comparison. For example, happiness may be a warm puppy to Charles Schultz and to many middle-class Americans, but to refugees from a war-torn country, happiness may be more like an elusive butterfly.

2. Metaphors are *structured*. They have a pattern that is shared between the items being compared. Earlier we looked at the pattern or structure of the likeness between the brain and a sponge. Perhaps you think the overall comparison of these two items is weak. Examine the structure in the comparison between happiness and a warm puppy. If in your experience happiness is lively, warm, wriggly, unrestrained, and bouncy, then comparing happiness to a puppy might make sense on the basis of this common pattern of attributes. If, however, you have experienced happiness as a more fragile feeling, it might not. Or if you have experienced puppies as messy, undisciplined, yappy, smelly, and full of fleas, you and Schultz might have difficulty reaching agreement on this metaphor.

3. Metaphors have *relationships* within their structures. For example, the properties of absorption, shape, and desiccation all show a relationship between the brain and a sponge. If you are unsatisfied with this metaphor, perhaps it is because the relationships break down. For example, the passivity of a sponge soaking up liquid may not agree with your notion of the selective activity of the brain.

4. Metaphors are *defined* in terms of our natural experiences. This definition differs from grounding in that these defining experiences are our most fundamental physical experiences starting from birth. They include perceptions, motor skills, cognition, and emotions. They are evoked by our interactions with the environment, such as movement, as in "exercise your prerogatives"; manipulating objects, as in "picking up on someone's ideas"; and eating, as in "he was a voracious reader."

In this book we modify Lakoff and Johnson's fourfold framework to clarify the elements for our purposes. We use the term *form* instead of *structure* to describe the general aspect of a comparison. We use *correspondence* instead of *relationship* to describe its internal complexity. And we use *connotation* instead of *definition* to emphasize the affective meaning characteristic of metaphors.

Grounding

The grounding of each metaphor in a particular set of experiences points to the importance of prior knowledge in understanding metaphors. For example, if we speak of someone's personality as being as warm and comfortable as Grandpa's old patched sweater, those who have had experiences with kind grandfathers and comfortable old sweaters will best appreciate the metaphor. Others who have been told about these things can understand, but may not be impressed. People from regions such as the tropics, where sweaters are not common garments, may be quite puzzled.

Form

Form relates to the general commonality of the two concepts involved and is usually what immediately strikes one about a metaphor. For example, in a comparison of the atom and the solar system, we need an overall picture of objects orbiting around a center. To entertain the metaphor that teaching is gardening, we need a structural picture of cultivation resulting in independent growth. The form may also be conceptual. The metaphor "iron curtain" requires a grasp of paradox, because one term seemingly contradicts the other: iron is hard and inflexible, whereas a curtain is usually soft and pliable. To combine them is to pose an anomaly and to heighten the threat of the phenomenon, which was the effect of the metaphor when it was first used.

Correspondences

Correspondences occur within the form of the metaphor. They are the multiple points of comparison within the form, and it is through these correspondences that we see the working of the metaphor. The more correspondences we can perceive, the more complex and convincing the metaphor; thus, the better the metaphor works. As an example, Howard A. Peele develops this metaphor for the term *metaphors*, which contains a number of correspondences:

> Metaphors cultivate the mind. They prepare furrows for planting ideas, which in time grow to mature understanding. If the climate is too arid for learning or if work has been neglected for too long, metaphors can break through an unreceptive crust to more fertile ground where the nutrients of teaching can be absorbed. (1984, 2)

Within the context of gardening, Peele brings out many correspondences: cultivation, planting, growth, climate, fertility, and nutrition. This metaphor, we might say, walks on many legs, not just one or two, but at least six.

Connotation

Metaphors themselves become definitions of our experience, and as Lakoff and Johnson point out, primary experiences are physical. We know the world first through our bodies. From that center, we move outward into social, political, and religious realms. In other words, metaphors express our attitudes, the connotative meanings that phenomena have for us both physically and socially.

For example, let us examine the metaphor that the teacher is a candle. This metaphor implies that the teacher's life is consumed by providing illumination for others. This is a Malaysian metaphor that captures the attitude toward teachers in that culture, where the word for teacher is *guru*. The candle metaphor expresses the ideal that dedicated teachers expend their life forces as energy in the transference of wisdom.

We might ask ourselves the extent to which this metaphor is appropriate to American culture. Do we, for example, have the same idea of teaching as self-sacrifice? We must consider the form and correspondences of the metaphor, and what these connote, in order to answer this question. To us the candle image may connote teacher burnout, which is probably not a connotation in the Malaysian metaphor.

Identifying the Basic Elements of Metaphors

Discuss each of the following metaphors with students in terms of its grounding, form, correspondences, and connotation. Some possible questions are listed for the first two metaphors.

1. "Binoculars work the way memory does. They compress space the way memory compresses time. You're looking out over a great distance, and yet everything seems close, and all the important images are in focus." (Robert Dufresne, "To Save a Life," in *The Way That Water Enters Stone*)

   Grounding: What experiences have you had looking through binoculars? Do you agree with the image that binoculars "compress space"?

   Form: Do binoculars do to space what memory does to time? What comparison between time and space does this analogy imply? Does it make sense to you?

   Correspondences: What are some ways in which binoculars seem to compress space? Do they make faraway things seem close up? Do they distort spatial perception? What are the effects of such compression on time? Can you remember something that happened years ago as if it were yesterday? Does this happen with all memories? What kinds of distortions may be involved in such memories?

   Connotation: What is the connotation of this metaphor? Does Dufresne mean that you can use your memory in the same way as you use a pair of binoculars? Does the metaphor refer equally to all stages of life or seem more applicable to people with a long history? What are some other circumstances in which you might imagine the metaphor applied?

2. "Technology is like genetic material. It is encoded with the characteristics of the society which developed it, and it tries to reproduce that society." (Bruno Wambi, "Carnival Called Science")

   Grounding: What is technology and what is genetic material?

   Form: How are technology and genetic material alike? Do you agree that each is encoded with traits of that which produced it?

   Correspondences: If you develop the idea of encoded traits of the parent organism or culture in both genetic material and technology, what do you find is reproduced by technology? Would you say that the correspondence holds in cases of transportation technology? agricultural technology? communications technology? war technology?

Connotation: What does the metaphor suggest about the nature of technology and its role in intercultural or intersocietal relationships? What does it say about exportation of technology from one country to another?

3. "Prose is a museum where all the old weapons of poetry are kept." (T. E. Hulme, *Speculations: Essays on Humanism and the Philosophy of Art*)

4. "Like a shrew eats, Nathan talked, as though, because of the nature of his metabolism, if he stopped for a few hours he would die." (David Quammen, "Nathan's Rime," in *Blood Line: Stories of Fathers and Sons*)

5. "His mind bred vermin. His thoughts were lice born of the sweat of sloth." (James Joyce, *Portrait of the Artist as a Young Man*)

6. "I am . . . telling you that we are connected to [animals] at least as intimately as we are connected to trees. Without plant life human beings could not breathe. Plants produce oxygen. Without free animal life I believe we will lose the spiritual equivalent of oxygen." (Alice Walker, *Living by the Word*)

7. "I returned and saw under the sun, that the race is not to the swift, nor the battle to the strong, neither yet bread to the wise, nor yet riches to men of understanding, nor yet favor to men of skill; but time and chance happeneth to them all." (Ecclesiastes)

Trying It Out

Metaphors from Sports: What's Your Game?

Many common expressions that we use today have their origins in various games or sports, though these sources may not be apparent in usage now. Shakespeare himself drew many expressions from sports. When Hamlet, in his famous soliloquy, said, "Aye, there's the rub," he was referring to the game of bowls or bowling, a "rub" being any obstruction impeding the roll of the ball. When Lady Macbeth urged her reluctant husband to "screw your courage to the sticking place," the reference was to tightening the string of the bow in archery.

The expressions listed in Table 1 all come from sports (Palmatier and Ray 1989), although they are likely to have lost that association in contemporary usage. Students will be able to find more examples. Using an unabridged or etymological dictionary, they can trace the origins of these metaphors as well as identify the components of grounding, form, correspondences, and connotations.

Term	Sport	Original Meaning
Rat race	Sailing	A dangerous tidal current, literally a "tide race"
Take a rain check	Baseball	Get a postponement ticket for a rained-out game
Shoo-in	Horse racing	A horse bound to win because the other jockeys had bet on it and were holding their horses back
Slush fund	Sailing	A fund accumulated by sailors from sale of excess grease or fat
Flat out	Auto racing	To go at full speed by putting the accelerator flat to the floor
Right up your alley	Baseball	To be in the part of the outfield that lies between fielders
Flash in the pan	Shooting	A flash of powder in a flintlock musket not accompanied by an explosion
Have a lark	Any contest	The word *lac* in Old English meant "contest" or "game"; hence, a good time
More than one way to skin a cat	Gymnastics	Refers to the maneuver of hanging by the bars and passing one's body between one's arms, which can be done forward or backward
Fluke	Billiards	A lucky shot
Tit for tat	Boxing	Blow for blow
Dead ringer	Horse racing, horseshoe pitching	A look-alike horse substituted for one of higher quality; a perfect horseshoe pitch that rings on the stake and lies touching it, hence one that looks like every other perfect throw
Knuckle under	Marbles	Yield to opponent's demand to shoot hand up with knuckles on the ground
Standoffish	Sailing	A standoff boat is one that stops short of coming to shore
Rapture	Falconry	The feeling of being seized and carried away by a bird of prey or "raptor"
In the nick of time	Soccer	Referring to the old custom of keeping score by notching a stick, a last-minute score

3 Kinds of Comparison Involved in Metaphorical Thinking

Metaphors open up virtually endless possibilities of comparison, giving words a chance to be more than words, offering the mind's eye a challenge to keep up with the fertile and articulate imagination of writers who make it their business to see things that ordinary people miss, noticing the most surprising likenesses.

Carl E. Bain et al., *The Norton Introduction to Literature*

What, in the wide range of possible kinds of comparison, shall we consider metaphor? For example, it is common to distinguish between *metaphor* and *simile*, the latter being an explicit comparison while the former is implicit. This distinction is a valid and important one. William A. Geiger, Jr. (1981), argues strongly for distinguishing implicit transfer, which he believes is more powerful in that it asserts that differences and similarities exist simultaneously. Nevertheless, in this book we set aside the distinction in favor of a broad conception of metaphor (a choice that Aristotle also made) in order to put emphasis on the imaginative use of comparison in various forms.

Maintaining Geiger's distinction can be cumbersome or inhibiting. If a student finds or produces a striking comparison, we do not want to reject it because of the presence of the words *like* or *as*. Moreover, in extended metaphors, explicit and implicit comparisons are often mixed. Consider, for example, R. L. Wing's explanation of the concept of the *tao* in Chinese philosophy:

> The *tao* literally means the way or gate through which all things move. To move with the *tao* is to be in a state that Christianity refers to as "grace." The Chinese philosophers were fond of comparing the *taoist* behavior with that of water: It flows onward always. It penetrates the crevices, it wears down resistance, it stops to fill deep places and then flows on. Always it holds to its true nature and always it flows with the forces in the cosmos. (1979, 12)

We immediately recognize the metaphor of "way" as a spiritual path and "gate" as an initiation to spiritual life. When Wing makes explicit the comparison between moving water and taoist behavior, he does not reduce the metaphorical impact of the passage. The implications of the water image go beyond explaining the concept of the tao and seem to suggest keeping up one's perseverance in a difficult situation.

Trying It Out

What's It Like? Similes

As a kind of limbering-up exercise, the following potential similes may elicit plausible comparisons. Students then can develop the possible images, or they can make up their own similes.

1. What is as . . .

   unpremeditated as a sneeze?

   irrevocable as a haircut?

   unfortunate as a centipede with athlete's foot?

   mutable as the price of gas?

   useless as a clock in a coffin?

   seedy as a raspberry?

   hard-boiled as an Easter egg?

   useless as a glass eye in a keyhole?

   lonely as a park bench in winter?

   elusive as a fish?

   sinful as chocolate cheesecake?

   virtuous as a grapefruit?

   tenacious as a cobweb?

   redundant as a thesaurus?

   predictable as a calendar?

2. What is like . . .

   walking naked among cannibals?

   scratching where there is no itch?

   winding an electric clock?

   trying to blow out a light bulb?

   two bad artists admiring each other's work?

   walking up the down escalator?

   trying to unscramble eggs?

   a modest peacock?

dieting for two weeks and gaining five pounds?

licking jelly from a sharp knife?

herding cats?

reading a letter in a dream?

looking at dew and seeing diamonds?

counting the feathers in a pillow?

shoveling smoke?

Synecdoche and Metonymy

A special kind of metaphor is one in which a part stands for the whole, as when an intelligent student is called a "brain," or a farmworker is called a "hand." Hopi Indians used to call Navajos "foreheads," because they brushed their hair back instead of wearing bangs as the Hopis did. Conversely, the whole may stand for a part, as in the expression "the law" for a police officer. The technical term for this figurative language is *synecdoche*.

Similarly, *metonymy* is the use of an associated notion to stand for a complex phenomenon. For example, in a community where there is a university, people not associated with the institution may be called "the town" and the people associated with it "the gown," referring to academic robes. Clothing is a common source of metonymy, as in "jocks" for athletes, "skirts" for females, "hardhats" for construction workers, "white collars" for people who work in offices, and "blue collars" for people who work in factories. The word "leathernecks" for Marines comes from a feature of their uniforms in the nineteenth century, when Marines had strong leather collars as protection against sword wounds.

Personification

Personification—ascribing human qualities to other species, inanimate objects, and ideas—is often a way of dramatizing a relationship that might otherwise be difficult to describe. In the following passage from *Walden*, Thoreau uses personification to convey the experience of growing beans on a plot of land that he has claimed from the wilderness:

> Removing the weeds, putting fresh soil about the bean stems, and encouraging this weed which I had sown, making the yellow soil express its summer thought in bean leaves and blossoms rather than in wormwood and piper and millet grass, making the earth say beans instead of grass,—this was my work. (1948, 134)

In the following dialogue, humorist Roy Blount, Jr., elaborates on the personification metaphor in the phrase "listen to your body."

> I was standing in the kitchen last evening, about six o'clock, and my tastebuds were clamoring, "Spaghetti! Spaghetti! With a whole lot of homemade sauce with hamburger and mushrooms and peppers and onions and Parmesan cheese! Come on! Can we? Pleeeeze?"
>
> And my mind was saying, "Wellll . . ."
>
> And my stomach was saying, "I'm not so sure."
>
> And my going-to-the-trouble-of-cooking muscles were saying, "Nahhh . . ."
>
> And my conscience was saying, "Raw carrots! Raw carrots!"
>
> And all of a sudden several parts of my body, in one voice, said, "How about a nice glass of bourbon with some ice in it?"
>
> "No," I said. "We're not going to drink. We've got too much work to do." (1989, 34)

In this example of personification, the underlying metaphor is that the conflicting desires and motivations we often experience, particularly between immediate and delayed gratification, are different individuals competing for attention.

In the following passage, author Lorrie Moore also uses personification to describe feelings, in this case the way a woman feels about her New York apartment, which is a beauty parlor converted into a loft, and the dislike she is beginning to feel for her husband:

> [S]he hated this place. But you could live with a hate. She had. It was so powerful, it had manners; it moved to one side most of the time to let you pass. It was mere dislike that clouded and nagged and stepped in front of your spirit, like a child wanting something. (1990, 162).

Puns and Homonyms

Question: What is a metaphor?

Answer: It's a place to put cows.

And what is a *pun* but an aural metaphor, the use of the sound of one word to evoke the meaning of another? Puns often appear in the form of riddles:

> Why did the lobster turn red? (Because he saw the salad dressing)
>
> What do you get when you cross a cantaloupe with a dog? (A melon collie)

Puns result from *homonyms*, words that sound similar or the same, but that have different meanings. In one common type of pun, the sound of a foreign word is revised to fit the sound of a native word. For example, the expression "raining cats and dogs" is thought to be an Anglicization of the Greek word *catadupa* meaning "cataract" (Radford 1973). The image of a waterfall is a more reasonable representation of a downpour than a shower of small pets.

Lewis Carroll created some of the most famous puns in the English language, and most teachers will remember the Mock Turtle's description of his "regular course" of studies at the bottom of the sea in *Alice's Adventures in Wonderland*:

> "What was that?" enquired Alice.
> "Reeling and Writhing, of course, to begin with," the Mock Turtle replied; "and then the different branches of Arithmetic—Ambition, Distraction, Uglification, and Derision." (1978, 76)

After a short discussion of these subjects, he continues telling Alice what else he learned:

> "Well, there was Mystery," the Mock Turtle replied, counting off the subjects on his flappers, "—Mystery, ancient and modern, with Seaography: then Drawling—the Drawling-master was an old conger-eel, that used to come once a week: *he* taught us Drawling, Stretching, and Fainting in Coils." (77)

The Gryphon then remarks that he went to the Classical master, "an old crab," to which the Mock Turtle soberly replies, "he taught Laughing and Grief, they used to say" (77).

A twentieth-century teacher of a similar bent, asked to bring in his scope-and-sequence plan for the next grading period, presented his department chair with a bottle of Scope mouthwash with sequins glued on it.

Punning is also an active ingredient in parody, as these titles of parodies indicate:

> "The Salad at the Bad Cafe" (J. MacClaren-Ross's parody of Carson McCullers's "The Ballad of the Sad Cafe")
>
> "Requiem for a Noun" (Peter De Vries's parody of William Faulkner's *Requiem for a Nun*)
>
> "Catch Her in the Oatmeal" (Dan Greenburg's Goldilocks parody of J. D. Salinger's *Catcher in the Rye*)

Malapropisms

Malapropism means an inappropriately used word, often chosen on the basis of a sound similarity to the appropriate one. In *Anguished English: An Anthology of Accidental Assaults upon Our Language*, Richard Lederer (1987) has published a collection of humorous student bloopers contributed by teachers from all over the United States. These bloopers range from calling the first book of the Bible

"Guinessis" and calling *The Odyssey* the "Oddity," to saying that Sir Francis Drake "circumcised" the world with a 100-foot clipper. Some inventive spellings also fall into this category, as Lederer points out: "Pullet Surprise" for Pulitzer Prize and "Donkey Hote" for Don Quixote. New spellings have also evolved into new words, as William Espy (1981) has noted. *An ewt* became *a newt*, the name we now give to the small lizard, and moving in the other direction, *a napron* became *an apron*.

Trying It Out

The Importance of Ambiguity

"Be precise," we often say to our students, but language is always eluding our efforts at precision. Words are constantly changing. We never know what new meaning a word may acquire, or what old meanings it may have left behind. The words *pane* and *panel*, for example, both started out meaning "a piece of cloth" (preserved still in the old-fashioned word for bedspread, *counterpane*). But they parted company in the fifteenth century to accommodate developments in architectural design and materials. One became transparent while the other became opaque.

Lewis Thomas praises this aspect of language as proof of its living nature. We are, he argues, "programmed to drift away in the presence of locked-on information, straying from each point in a hunt for a better, different point." It is this attraction to ambiguity, he claims, that constitutes the uniqueness of human thought:

> If it were not for the capacity for ambiguity, for the sensing of strangeness, that words in all languages provide, we would have no way of recognizing the layers of counterpoint in meaning, and we might be spending all our time sitting on stone fences, staring into the sun. To be sure, we would always have had some everyday use to make of the alphabet, and we might have reached the same capacity for small talk, but it is unlikely that we would have been able to evolve from words to Bach. The great thing about human language is that it prevents us from sticking to the matter at hand. (1974, 111–12)

Philip Howard (1988) has coined the term "Janus word," based on the Roman god depicted with two faces looking in opposite directions, to indicate a word or phrase with meanings that seem to contradict each other, such as the following examples:

| **To cleave**: | To split apart | $\longleftrightarrow$ | To cling to |
| **Fast**: | Quickly, speedily | $\longleftrightarrow$ | Stationary, kept from moving |

Mortar:	Material for sticking things together	⟷	A device for blowing things apart
Throw out:	Provide (I'll throw out this idea for the group)	⟷	Dispose of (If you don't like this idea, you can throw it out)
Sanction:	Give permission, approve	⟷	Deny, disapprove

Ask students to search for their own pairs of Janus words or terms with contradictory meanings. Looking up the ambiguities may reveal the words' metaphorical stories.

Synesthesia

Being such liberating devices, metaphors can also help us transcend the limits of sensory consistency. Poets often use the device of *synesthesia*, or sensory crossover, to dramatic effect: Goethe's definition of architecture as "frozen music," or Alfred Bruemeau's description of music as "cathedrals in sound." The images in such statements as "I felt his gaze upon me," "I saw the pain in her expression," and "You are a feast for the eyes" are metaphorical, but they are so commonly used that we no longer respond to them as such. Other images, such as "I heard a tall, brunette voice" or "Her L. L. Bean jacket resonated with his Pendleton shirt," might get our attention, but we still might not consciously attend to the sensory crossovers involved. The effectiveness of synesthesia as a figurative device often lies in its subtlety.

Trying It Out

Senses on Overload: Synesthesia

Webster's *New World Dictionary* (Third College Edition, 1988) defines *synesthesia* as "a process in which one type of stimulus produces a secondary, subjective sensation as when some color evokes a specific smell." This is a minimal way of describing the possibilities of linking the experiences of the senses.

Activity 1

Bring to class an assortment of items for evoking various senses, such as the following:

a record or tape with sound effects (e.g., train, wind, rain)

something to be touched, with a definite feel (such as wetness or texture), placed unseen in a closed container

a large piece of paper or material of a vivid color

something with a distinct taste (if possible, unrecognizable), such as cardamom seeds or an unusual flavoring

something with a distinct odor, also in a container, such as an unfamiliar spice

Present one item at a time to the class. Let everyone hear, touch, see, taste, or smell as appropriate. Students write down their descriptions of each item, using senses other than the primary one. For example, to generate synesthetic descriptions of a sound, they can ask themselves how it would feel, how it would taste, how it would look, and how it would smell.

Activity 2

Students meet in small groups to compare their descriptions and to decide on three or four good responses to each item. List these on the board.

Students arrange the sensory words for each item in a way that seems coherent to them; for example, the red of the cloth is harsh, spicy, rough, and pungent. These clusters of metaphors can be compared across groups for connotations and overall images.

Activity 3

Share with students other examples of synesthesia from ordinary speech and literature, such as the following:

Scents that are "soft as oboes, green as meadows." (Charles Pierre Baudelaire, "Correspondences")

"The morning light creaks down again." (Edith Sitwell, "Aubade")

"A loud perfume." (John Donne, "Elegy IV: The Perfume")

As follow up, students can form free verses from the phrases they have collected and from other sources, working individually or in groups. Students can also bring in more examples of synesthesia and discuss the meanings and the effects of these images.

Oxymorons

Oscar Wilde, famous for his cynical wit, claimed that "punctuality is the thief of time." He also referred to a boring friend as not having "a single redeeming vice." The juxtaposition of the unexpected and seemingly contradictory in a way that paradoxically makes sense is known as *oxymoron*, derived from two Greek words with opposite meanings, "sharp" and "foolish." Well-known oxymorons include the titles of Paul Simon's song "The Sounds of Silence" and David Riesman's book *The Lonely Crowd*. Looked at metaphorically, "jumbo shrimp" is another example. The power of incongruity is evident in such phrases as "the sound of one hand clapping," "passive aggression," "the constancy of change," and

Victor Hugo's last words, "black light," a term that has now entered our technical vocabulary.

Narrative Metaphors

Stuart Hannabus (1987) cites Franz Kafka's famous bureaucracy metaphors of the castle and the trial and Hans Christian Andersen's metaphor of the emperor's new clothes as classics in social understanding. The plots of myths, allegories, and fairy tales, he argues, are ways of answering the larger questions that we must put to ourselves as humans: How do you win against odds? How do you recognize and cope with evil? These stories, which often unconsciously draw readers into multiple levels of understanding, are metaphors for basic issues in life.

Our commonest wisdom often comes from the animal kingdom, from which we have been drawing instructive metaphors throughout recorded history. "The early bird catches the worm," "Birds of a feather flock together," and "A bird in the hand is worth two in the bush" are samples of the extent to which we have enlightened ourselves from just one species. Fables and animal tales elaborate on metaphorical connections between humans and other animals: the sly but susceptible fox, the wicked but assailable wolf, the conscientious hen, the ingenuous chicken, the vain crow, the persistent turtle, and the erratic rabbit are models that, from our earliest childhood, help us understand ourselves and interpret others.

In her novel *Pitch Dark*, Renata Adler has created a contemporary fable based on the shrew:

> When I learned about the shrew, the poor unevolved, benighted shrew, which will keep jumping high in the air at a place in its accustomed path where an obstacle, a rock perhaps, once was but no longer is, well, I wondered about all those places where, though the obstacles have long been removed, one persists either in the jump or in taking the long way round. It seemed such an unnecessary jolt or expenditure of time and energy. And yet if you have acquired a profound aversion for just such a place simply because of an obstacle that once was there, or an incapacity to discern that the obstacle no longer exists, or an indifference as to whether it exists or not, or if the habit of pointless jumping, or detour, or even turning back dejected has become for you the path itself, or if you have a superstitious need to treat the spot as though the obstacle remained, or even a belief that the discovery that the obstacle is gone is in itself a punishable offense, if any of these things is true for you, then you are lost. Or probably lost, unless the habitual path, the compulsion, the leap, the turning back, the long detour have for you another value. Individuality, for instance, love, obsession. Or for that matter, art. (1983, 82–83)

This comparison takes us in different directions. The shrew's irrational behavior is a metaphor for human compulsion or learned inhibition, demonstrated in the responses to people who behave as if past obstacles are still present, and who therefore proceed inefficiently. For example, people who were once poor may never feel secure even though they have later achieved affluence. A writer who has received several rejection slips may avoid sending out more stories. A college student who was called dyslexic as a young child may still fear reading assignments, although the reading problem has long been resolved.

But then Adler suggests that, for very personal purposes, which may be more important than the practical ones, the seemingly irrational behavior might be quite appropriate. Holding onto the idea of one's former poverty may be an act of simplification that clarifies one's thoughts and frees one from the demands of wealth. Henry David Thoreau, settling for a hand-built cabin on Walden pond, turned away from ownership and congratulated himself for not having done damage to his poverty. Albert Einstein, deemed dyslexic, found elaborate alternative ways of finding answers to questions and thereby became one of the great thinkers of modern times. Emily Dickinson, virtually a recluse in her father's home, wrote poetry with the brilliance and cutting power of diamonds. What passes at a given time for common sense may not, Adler suggests, always be the most productive or desirable state of mind.

Trying It Out

Twisting the Tails of Animal Metaphors

In Renata Adler's extended metaphor of the shrew, reprinted above, we saw that she was going in one direction but then turned in another. A fable, or animal metaphor, need not be confined to one point. It can take a twist, that is, a surprise turn at the end that suggests alternative, even contradictory, interpretations to those conventionally assumed. Marianne Moore's poem about the fox and the grapes gives an example of such a twist:

The Fox and the Grapes

A fox of Gascon, though some say of Norman descent,
When starved till faint gazed up at a trellis to which grapes
    were tied.
    Matured till they glowed with a purplish tint
    As though there were gems inside.
Now grapes were what our adventurer on strained haunches
    chanced to crave.
    But because he could not reach the vine

He said, "These grapes are sour. I'll leave them for some knave."

Better, I think, than an embittered whine. (1982)

In the standard fable of the fox and the grapes, the fox is used to characterize a certain combination of human tendencies: desire, fallibility, and rationalization. The fable leads us to laugh at these qualities in ourselves and others, especially the tendency to reduce cognitive dissonance by saying we do not really want something we cannot have, or as the phrase has become immortalized, "Sour grapes!" Marianne Moore's poem, however, gives this tendency a heroic cast. Her poem suggests that it is better to put one's own positive interpretation on a hopeless situation than simply to sulk about what one cannot have.

Students can try extending the metaphors of other fables and adding a new twist. Working individually or in groups, they decide how to change the tone and intent of the fable. For example, in the fable "The Fox and the Crow," in which the fox gets the crow's cheese through flattery, the crow may be perceived as a poet who sacrifices life to art, whereas the fox is merely a materialistic opportunist. In "The Tortoise and the Hare," the hare may decide to drop out of the rat race and pursue other values in life while the tortoise continues his dogged pursuit of trivial achievements.

Analogy

Although a strict distinction between metaphors and analogies is not always made, *analogy* is often considered as more of a logical than an imaginative device. In this view the aim of analogy is not so much to link two disparate items in a creative manner as to find their structural or proportional similarity. The items on many verbal aptitude and critical thinking tests illustrate one frequent use of this concept of analogy. Analogy is frequently used in science to illustrate structural similarity. For example, a cornstalk can be shown to be like a flower in having analogous parts. A horse's hoof is analogous to a toenail. In the phrase "ontogeny recapitulates phylogeny," an analogy is drawn between the development of a fetus and the stages through which animal life has presumably passed to reach modern mammalian status.

Analogy is commonly defined as a resemblance between the relations of things, to which W. H. Leatherdale adds, "resemblance in an ensemble of qualities, . . . properties, or attributes." As examples he cites the following:

Galileo recognizing an analogy between the motion of an object dropped on a moving ship and projectile motion, . . . Newton seeing the moon, a heavenly body, as analogous to a terrestrial projectile, or . . . Darwin recognizing the competition for survival in nature is analogous in its effects to selective breeding under domestication. (1974, 16)

Analogies embody perceptions of logical correspondences and may seem to emphasize structure over connotation. In many respects, however, analogies are much the same as metaphors. The historical development of physicists' conceptions of the atom has moved through a series of analogies that are also metaphors: the billiard ball model, the plum pudding model, the planetary model, and the orbital model, in which the emphasis is on the electron's motion rather than its position: an atom is like a miniature solar system in that electrons orbit a nucleus the way planets orbit the sun. This statement is not so much analogically precise as it is imagistic and insightful. It does not reveal a specific underlying structure in the same way that "1:3 :: 3:9" or "a wing is analogous to a hand" do. But it does provide the metaphorical bridge from knowledge in one context to knowledge in another. And like the ontogeny analogy above, it implies the possibility of more profound knowledge about the nature of things yet to be disclosed. Leatherdale tells the following story to illustrate the role analogical thinking often plays in scientific discovery:

> When Mayer bled a sailor who fell on the ship on which he was a medical officer, it was the analogy between the brighter redness than usual of the venous blood in the tropics and the usual colour of arterial blood that led him, via the idea that metabolism drew less oxygen from the blood in hot climates because maintenance of body temperature required less heat, to a lifelong interest in the conservation of energy, of which concept he was a pioneer. Again, the analogy which led to Bradley's explanation of the aberration of light depended upon the imported analogue of the movement of a flag on the mast of a sailing ship as it changed tack; a very far cry from the astronomical problems which Bradley was trying to solve. (18)

Similarly, Leonardo da Vinci designed the prototype for an airplane after observing the flight of birds. By studying the membrane of the ear, Alexander Bell was able to design a similar membrane for the telephone. Analogies have affected our lives in many ways.

Symbols

Symbols are stylized representations that have attained some permanence of meaning and therefore a stable role in a culture's communications system. A symbol may or may not be metaphorical in the sense of being based on an actual comparison. For example, a red light is a commonly recognized symbol for "stop" and a green light for "go," but there is no actual similarity between the colors and the actions. A wedding ring, on the other hand, can be viewed as bearing a resemblance to what it symbolizes, the closed bond of marriage. Metaphorically establishing symbols is at the heart of literature, in that elements often go beyond their common meanings to suggest a universality that draws readers into the literary experience. Describing a face as "innocent as a cabbage" treats the cabbage as a symbol of naiveté, while saying a face "buries itself like a hatchet in someone's neck" makes the hatchet a symbol of sudden attack.

Jack Solomon discusses the metaphorical basis of two of our most powerful symbols of wealth, silver and gold:

> Gold and silver became precious in the ancient world because of their *resemblance* to other precious things: gold, to the brightness of the sun that rises every morning and returns with renewed strength every spring to begin a new season of growth; and silver, to the brightness of the moon that waxes and wanes through the months, associated in the ancient world with feminine fertility. More importantly, gold, which neither rusts nor tarnishes, resembles unchanging, incorruptible immortality itself. (1988, 51)

The conception of metaphor adopted here, then, is a broad one, including such variations as simile, metonymy, synecdoche, personification, synesthesia, oxymoron, narrative comparisons such as fables and allegories, analogy, and symbol. Without denying the importance of the distinctions among these types of figurative speech, which may be crucial in some contexts, here we are focusing on their common essence, the notion of imaginative comparison.

Trying It Out

Colorful Metaphors

One of the first things that parents teach their children is to identify colors. It is no wonder that there are many metaphors linked with color.

I saw red!

She's feeling blue.

He has a yellow streak.

The associations with color are so strong that the reader registers these statements in order as anger, melancholy, and cowardice, without thinking of the color-as-metaphor aspect in figurative language. Color metaphors that denote moods can be traced back to medieval physiology, when the four humors were considered responsible for one's well-being and temperament.

Humor	Temperament	Color	Quality
blood	sanguine	red	hot-moist
yellow bile	choleric	yellow	hot-dry
black bile	melancholic	black	cold-dry
phlegm	phlegmatic	white	cold-moist

It is from medieval reasoning that expressions like "lily-livered," "green with envy," and "red-hot lover" were derived to explain someone's disposition.

Colors have different meanings depending on our cultural perspective. In Western cultures, white is the traditional color for brides, and black is the color for funerals; but in India, white is associated with funerals, and red is worn at weddings. Students may wish to explore such differences in color symbolism across cultures.

Activities

Students brainstorm common color metaphors that would denote feelings or dispositions; for example, "She argued till she was blue in the face." Point out passages in literature in which color metaphors are used, such as this passage from Shakespeare's *Romeo and Juliet*:

> But soft! What light through yonder window breaks?
> It is the East, and Juliet is the sun!
> Arise, fair sun, and kill the envious moon,
> Who is already sick and pale with grief
> That thou her maid art more fair than she.
> Be not her maid, since she is envious.
> Her vestal livery is but sick and green,
> And none but fools do wear it. Cast it off.
> (Act II, scene 2, lines 2–9)

Before students write their own color metaphors, they might examine some of our other associations with color, some linked to mood, some not. Ask students to respond to different colors: "What do you think of or associate with the color green?" For example, green is nature. It may conjure up images of Robin Hood or Girl Scouts. Green is supposed to be a relaxing color; hence, before a performance, actors would wait in a backstage room that was painted green and called "the green room." This theatrical usage has been applied in television studios so that talk-show guests wait in an area designated as "the green room," whether or not it is actually painted green. Green is also a metaphor for illness, a meaning quite opposed to that of relaxation. Cartoons sometimes show a person inhaling the smoke from a first cigarette and then turning green.

Colors have become metaphors for many things in our society. White is the purity of an angel and the antiseptic nurse. Purple is royalty. Colors have become part of our traffic system. Red stops us and warns of danger, yellow cautions us, green releases us to continue on our way.

Here is another reference to color in a metaphor-laden passage from Tom Wolfe's *Bonfire of the Vanities:*

> Sherman's attention was drawn to a bouquet of ecstatic boiling faces in the immediate foreground. Two men and an impeccably emaciated woman were grinning upon a huge young man with pale blond hair and a cowlick at the top of his forehead . . . *Met him somewhere . . . but who is he? . . . Bango!* . . . Another face from the press . . . The Golden Hillbilly, the Towheaded Tenor . . . That was what they called him . . . His name was Bobby Shaflett. He was the new featured tenor of the Metropolitan Opera, a grossly fat creature who had somehow emerged from the upland hollows of the Appalachians. (1987, 348)

After exploring the many ramifications of color in our culture, students can then write their own color metaphors. Invite them to share their metaphors and to discuss what moods the metaphors convey and perhaps what historical or social references they may contain.

II Personal and Cultural Aspects of Metaphors

4 Metaphors and Self-Awareness

I am something real and really existing, but what thing am I? I have already given the answer: a thing which thinks. And what more? I will stimulate my imagination (to see if I am not something else beyond this). I am not this assemblage of members which is called a human body; I am not a rarefied and penetrating air spread throughout all these members; I am not a wind, (a flame) a breath, a vapor, or anything at all that I can imagine and picture to myself since I have supposed that all that was nothing, and since without abandoning this supposition, I find that I do not cease to be certain that I am something.

René Descartes, *Discourse on Method and Meditations*

Almost from birth, we have been consciously and unconsciously building a system of metaphors that explains ourselves to ourselves in three ways. First, we hear what others say about us, basically because we cannot do much but listen at that early time in our lives. Second, we explain ourselves to ourselves. Third, we explain ourselves to others. As we grow older, these three systems of metaphors so intertwine within our mental structure that they dictate who we are, what we think, what we say, and how we behave. They, in fact, create our subjective sense of who we are.

Let us begin with metaphors for ourselves that others formulate. When we are brought home from the hospital, and sweet Aunt May bends over our crib and says, "What a little doll baby!" we begin with that first metaphor in our mental substructure. (That is not to say that we understand the concept of "baby," or "doll," but others have started a substructure in their minds including that greeting, which will be imprinted upon us piece by piece, time after time.) Our awareness of ourselves has begun with the cooing sound of a well-meaning (if we are lucky), possibly doting aunt. Metaphors such as "brat," "hindrance," or "excess baggage" added to our substructure not only hurt but also last longer, with perhaps even stronger effects than "baby" or "doll."

Over time, we build a collection of metaphors that others have used to describe us, and we of little worldly knowledge and simple faith in others tend to believe all or most of what we are told. It is often observed that play is a rehearsal for adult life, and the roles that children enact reflect the seeds that have been planted concerning who they are. Children who consider themselves "brains," "troublemakers," "jocks," "little ladies," "gentlemen," or "outcasts" are molding themselves to these images. These mental collections of self-metaphors are all there, and at an early age they are already imprinted.

The metaphors that children use to describe themselves and others are very revealing of their conceptions of the world and their place in it. The following inventory of adolescent social types was compiled by a thirteen-year-old after polling ten of his friends:

> **Skater**—wears "Bugle Boy" clothing, rides a skateboard, and usually has an intense opinion about whatever is going on, displays a distinct "attitude."
>
> **Grit**—dirty, mean people
>
> **Yuppie**—doesn't work, lives off parents' income, wears "good" clothes.
>
> **Pozer**—looks like one of the other categories (mainly skater) but isn't really.
>
> **Skinhead**—rebel, thinks he is pro-communist but doesn't know what one is, wants to be different.
>
> **Homeboy**—"Nerd" that stays home and plays video games alone.
>
> **Jock**—an athletic Yuppie
>
> **Headbanger**—town "Grit," only more excitable, and always wears black.

As L. S. Vygotsky (1978) proposed, our sense of self is internalized from the messages we receive from others. In this kind of categorizing, individuals receive the social definitions from which they will fashion their identities. This powerful role of language is one that deserves our critical attention.

We also set up a system of how we view others. The metaphors that we use when we are thinking or speaking of others represent our feelings regarding that person. Listen to another teacher describe a student you know, and compare your image to the one the other teacher has. Sometimes the two match perfectly, while at other times you wonder if the two of you are talking about the same person. The disagreement is likely to be expressed through the metaphors the two teachers use to describe the student. The next time you are involved in a discussion with other teachers, pay critical attention to the metaphors you use and hear. This easy kind of discourse analysis can reveal a great deal about the power of metaphors.

Another way to examine metaphoric power is to complete

the sentence: "Teaching is like. . . ." If your metaphor is something like "pulling teeth" or "storming the Bastille," you may want to think about why you are actually in this profession. (On the other hand, maybe you are merely tired or having a bad day!) Or you may think that teaching is like planting seeds and cultivating the young plants that appear. Being aware of the metaphors that we use, especially the ones we think and use repeatedly, indicates our true feelings about issues, events, and people. Sometimes these powerful images need to be recognized and reevaluated.

Trying It Out

Metaphors for Learning

Of obvious importance to students is the development of metaphors that help them educationally and that instill values that will be supportive of notions of lifelong learning. Understanding and controlling their own learning processes will give students power over their fates, immediate and long term.

Activity 1

Discuss the following common metaphors for learners with your students. Ask them to consider the grounding, form, correspondences, and connotations of each of these examples. Then have them choose and/or develop metaphors that they find productive for themselves.

> *Lump of Clay*: One metaphor to explain the educational process is that the learner is like a lump of clay, warmed by attention and concern, slowly and carefully molded into a mature thinker. However, one must be careful with this material because it crumbles when handled roughly and does not stand up well under stress. It can also be messy. Accepting this metaphor implies the belief that cognitive development is primarily shaped from the outside, through the environment. The metaphor may break down for some people in some of its connotations, e.g., a lump of clay seems dense and without feeling, and it is wholly passive, lacking any individual tendencies or even the ability to act.

> *Rosebush*: One may therefore prefer the metaphor of the rosebush, a special form of the gardening metaphor for education. With proper fertilizer, sunlight, and water, the rosebush will grow and bring forth its characteristic flower. The promise of the rosebush is the learner's own, but it requires external care to be realized. This care will help the bush reach its inherent potential, but it cannot change its essential nature. No amount of cultivation can change a pink rambling rose into a red American Beauty. When appreciated for itself, however, the small rose, like the larger rose, can attain its full measure of beauty. This metaphor may have advantages over

the lump-of-clay metaphor, even though the aspects of emotion, volition, thought, and social consciousness are not yet addressed.

Activity 2 Discuss the following two metaphors for learners, noting their very different connotations. Ask students to consider the implications that the metaphors convey regarding the learner as active or passive.

> A learner is a voyager starting out on a journey.
>
> A learner is a vessel to be filled with knowledge and wisdom.

Activity 3 Ask students to think of their own metaphors for learners. These metaphors should emphasize attributes that they consider important, especially in themselves. The following questions and comments might guide the students' discussion of their metaphors:

- Are you like a sponge, so you would like teachers to give you as much information as possible to soak up?
- Are you like a bird waiting to try your wings to fly?
- Or are you like a young tree, small now but with great potential, so you would like to be given light, nourishment, and room to grow without being cut down?

By using their imaginations, students can come up with unique characterizations of themselves as learners, which will help them understand and communicate themselves to others.

Trying It Out

Reflections of Ourselves: Examining Self-Metaphors

The images we hold of ourselves become apparent through our self-metaphors. As we become aware of the connection between language and self-image, we can begin to control the latter through manipulating the former. Students begin to understand this phenomenon first through observing the self-metaphors used by writers of all kinds and then by examining their own self-metaphors. Here are some well-known statements of self-definition by poets and song writers:

> I am the master of my fate;
> I am the captain of my soul.
>> William Ernest Henley, "Invictus"

> I'm a lean dog, a keen dog, a wild dog and lone,
> I'm a rough dog, a tough dog, hunting on my own!
> I'm a bad dog, a mad dog, teasing silly sheep. . . .
>> Irene Rutherford McLeod, "Lone Dog"

I am a rock, I am an island. . . .
  Paul Simon, "I Am a Rock"

I am woman, hear me roar. . . .
  Helen Reddy, "I Am Woman"

Activity 1   After discussing these and other self-metaphors, students write a paragraph on each of the following questions about themselves as they are right now:

- What animal best describes you? Why?
- What color best describes you? Why?
- What inanimate object best describes you? Why?
- What food best describes you? Why?

Students can also specify their own categories of comparison, such as season, holiday, or country.

Share and discuss the metaphors that students devise, putting special emphasis on the images and what these images suggest about writers' attitudes toward themselves. Some feelings may be universal, while others are unique to individuals. Convey to the students that both aspects are to be valued and that even the universal feelings vary in intensity from time to time.

From this beginning, a discussion of metaphors per se can evolve, guided perhaps by the following questions:

- How do we generate metaphors about ourselves?
- Are our several metaphors for ourselves always consistent with each other? Does it matter if they are not?
- What effects do our self-metaphors have on how we do the following:

    think about ourselves?

    relate to others?

    perform in school? at sports? during social interactions?

    choose our careers?

    dress and otherwise present ourselves?

- How and to what extent can we control our self-metaphors?

Activity 2   Students write other paragraphs on the animals, plants, colors, inanimate objects, foods, and other categories that they would *like* to be, and explain why. Share and discuss these images in class.

Activity 3   Students take the two sets of paragraphs produced in the first two activities, choose pairs of images that seem disparate (i.e., contain a discrepancy between how they see themselves as being now and how they would like to be), and write connecting paragraphs that describe how they can get from the present to the desired image. For example, a girl who first described herself as a wren might have chosen a swan as her ideal image; in the connecting paragraph she would describe mental changes that would allow her to get from the first to the second self-identity.

Students need not share these connecting paragraphs with the class, nor even with the teacher. The importance of this part of the exercise is for students to communicate intrapersonally about how to take control of the person they are becoming as they develop. The privacy of this internal conversation needs to be respected. Nevertheless, a general discussion on changing personal metaphors would be appropriate, perhaps with an example not drawn from the students' own papers, such as the following:

> *From Activity 1*: I am like a cup in a restaurant because I am used by everyone and have no particular identity of my own. Everyone forgets about me when I no longer serve their purpose.

> *From Activity 2*: I would like to be like a hand-cut crystal vase, unique, valuable, and cherished by someone.

> *From Activity 3*: To get from the first to the second image, I will reflect my own brightness, show others that I am significant, refuse to let people treat me like a common object, and do everything I can to feel proud of myself.

When an individual has a metaphor with which to practice positive self-imagery, that person's attitudes and actions can change significantly over time, affecting as well the attitudes and reactions of others. The principle is that we act out the roles we set for ourselves, but often we are not conscious of what we are doing. This exercise has been about awakening our consciousness of metaphor making.

Trying It Out

Metaphors and Self: A Letter to Myself

In this activity students explore various metaphorical ways of describing themselves and their environment as if they were writing to a stranger. The stranger, however, is themselves at some specified time in the future. Just as we can look back on our past selves as if they were other people who played crucial roles in our lives, so also can we look at our future selves as other people whose lives we are affecting. What can we say to these future people to make them understand who we are and what we are experiencing now?

In his account of diary writers, *A Book of One's Own: People and Their Diaries*, Thomas Mallon looks back on his own collection of diaries, comparing two passages written about a decade before. In the first, he was recording what he called "a rotten day, part of a rotten time":

> Now it's Christmas, and it might have been different . . . by luck perhaps . . . I would have a notebook full of my reflections on the pretty peeling blue wallpaper in my room, the funny way C . . . smokes a cigarette, the way the Boston subway smells, the afternoon a rainbow danced on M . . .'s forehead and hair as A . . . and I watched it . . . a thousand such reflections. All of it has happened, all of it has been seen, everything is the same— except—it has not been given a second thought. I am a computer which eats the cards and spews forth no print-out. I am eating up the raw material of life like some furnace, but I don't even give out bilge. No product. No process. Just feed.
>
> There's been a war, and Washington grinds on, and there's a great national bore called the energy crisis (1984, xi–xii).

He calls this "pretty self-pitying stuff," but reading it invokes his feelings of that night ten years earlier. Another observation that he makes is that previous to this entry he had neglected his diary for five months, which makes him angry at his past self for indulging in worries and not recording his experience. "I resented it all being wasted," he writes, "everything, from the peeling wallpaper to C . . .'s cigarettes to the rainbow on M . . .'s forehead. . . ." But less than a month later, he wrote this:

> One of those nights when, for a moment, I think: "A thousand years wouldn't be enough." A dusting of snow fell today, just enough to freshen the dirty pile on the ground: Nature's cosmetic. Once again each filament of bare branch is frosted . . . splendid lattices stretching under the lamps of the Yard and in front of the museum. No, a thousand years would not be enough to watch this. (xii)

From these entries, Mallon evokes his former self, "a figure now part of the past, available to be summoned." He is glad he sat down on both occasions to write. He could see this person in different dimensions and read his story, which was quite dramatic. The meaning and beauty of life that seemed missing in the first passage had been found in the second. The malfunctioning computer had become not only human, but also a sensitive observer of nature's cosmetics. Mallon demonstrates the insights we can gain in the present by knowing our own stories from the past.

Activity 1   Students read this passage on Mallon and think about the metaphors he uses. Ask them why he compares himself to a computer that eats punch cards (used by older computers instead of diskettes or internal drives), but that produces no printout? What do they think of his description of the snow on the branches in January? Again, he uses a metaphor, but a different kind from the one he used a few weeks earlier, reflecting a quite different state of mind. Discuss with students the implications of the metaphors. Why are they important to the older Mallon, who goes back to reread his ten-year-old diaries?

In rereading his entries, Mallon is glad that he wrote both down, and he is annoyed with himself for letting half a year go by without recording any observations. He had failed to "savor" this part of his life; he had "wasted" it. He also looks back on himself as another person, seeing "someone who, while he may not have achieved every dream, got what he was so bitter about missing. . . ." In these two excerpts, a narrative begins to unfold, with a plot and main character.

Activity 2   Students explore various ways of describing themselves and important aspects of their present environment. Encourage them to prepare vivid descriptions of their present feelings, mental state, ideas, and experiences. Such questions as the following may stimulate imaginative thinking (see also Carpenter 1988; Elbow 1981):

- What season are you most like?
- What time of day best describes you?
- Who or what could serve as your guardian spirit?
- What is the fragrance of your essence?
- What fairy tale or nursery rhyme tells your story the best?
- What character from literature or history do you identify with most?

Activity 3   Students imagine someone else picking up a diary or letter that they have written. What observations, feelings, fears, or desires do they think are most important to explain who they are?

Next, over a period of time (from one week to a semester or grading period), students keep a diary or write an extended letter to themselves in the future, specifying the time in the future and whether the letter will be open or closed to other readers in the class.

Students seal these letters or diaries to their future selves in dated envelopes and open them at the time specified. Or if the future date is soon enough, you might agree to mail the envelopes at the appropriate time. (If students provide about twice as much postage as current rates require, they will probably keep up with future inflation!) This is a risky alternative since much can happen to you or your students in the time intervening, especially if the interval is lengthy. But this approach heightens the drama of actually receiving a letter from oneself. Other arrangements might be to have a friend or relative keep the envelope until the specified time. The point is that the communication must be real and imaginatively written so that the future reader truly recalls and understands the content.

5 Metaphors and the Enabling Process

Hold fast to dreams
For if dreams die,
Life is a broken-winged bird
That can not fly.

Langston Hughes, "Dreams"

As was suggested earlier, metaphors can help or hinder one's ability to learn, develop, and achieve. Your role in helping students find metaphors that enable them to solve problems, develop self-esteem, and grow emotionally as well as intellectually is an enormously important part of your job as a teacher. Through enabling metaphors that you supply, students begin to visualize problems or concerns in new ways, thereby gaining new perspectives on them.

Enabling metaphors can help students aim higher, hang on longer, fight more strongly, and even fall less heavily. Quite often one is told to "look at the whole picture," suggesting how important we consider seeing as a way of understanding. Naming is also a powerful technique for gaining control. One of Ursula Le Guin's characters in her *Earthsea* books, Ced, is told to name his enemy or fear. Once named, the aversion can be encountered.

A teenage girl, confronting a bad relationship, created this metaphor:

You were my cancerous
All-consuming
habit.

By comparing the relationship to a cigarette habit and stating that ending it made her "feel healthier and better than before," she not only defined the problem, but she set up a thinking process that enabled her to decide alternatives. Some readers may recall the skit Ed Grimley did on "Saturday Night Live" in which he imagined himself as a man and as a mouse. This process of comparing alternatives, although confusing, is one that students could use to achieve greater clarity.

A powerful example of a young person's metaphorical thinking to see past the immediate situation involved Clara, a girl from a very restrictive, rule-bound family. This girl, described by Sherry Turkle in her book *The Second Self: Computers and the Human Spirit* (1984), used the concept of computer programming to describe herself, but rather than finding this a negative metaphor, she used it for self-liberation. If a person can be programmed in the first place, she reasoned, then that program can also be changed, something she knew she would have the option of doing later in life. Clara's experience with programming resulted in a metaphorical insight that gave her hope for the future.

One needs neither special experience nor an unusual metaphor to be enriched or liberated. Youngsters can gain new viewpoints even from such clichés as "Girls are like streetcars; if you miss one, another will come along," and "Boys are like fish in the sea; there are plenty more where he came from." "What if" speculations can also be productive in thinking one's way to a clearer understanding of one's situation. In the song "If I Were a Rich Man," Tevye in *Fiddler on the Roof* imagines himself to be something he is not and, by the end of the song, has changed his mind about his desire for unattainable wealth.

Enabling metaphors support many positive outcomes. Four important outcomes for teachers and students are *reassurance, endurance, mastery* over some problem or goal, and *philosophical values*, all described more fully below.

Reassurance

Such epigrams as "Learners are like flowers, unfolding in their own time," and "One must walk before one can run" may ease anxiety and enable students to continue their efforts at their own pace, even though others may advance more quickly. The singer Cyndi Lauper had a hit song called "True Colors" in which she compared her friends' attributes to the colors of the rainbow. The central image in this song confirmed the worth of each individual and conveyed the message that one's "colors," whether physical or metaphorical, need only be authentic.

Tonya Venstra, one of the authors of this volume, holds a fond memory of her father telling her that floating on water was like "sleeping on a cloud. . . . Not only was I able to relax and actually float, but to this day I still associate floating in water with clouds and a sense of belonging to the elements."

After making a bad dive from the lowest diving board of a municipal pool, a young man was so humiliated that he wanted to walk away. But someone reminded him of the adage about falling off a horse—unless you get right back on, you may never ride again. This reminder persuaded the young man that continuing to try again was more important than escaping the scene of embarrassment.

Metaphors from nature remind us of the cycles of life, reassuring us that "after the darkest hour comes the dawn" and that "if winter comes, spring cannot be far behind." The Hindu concept of karma is a metaphorical reassurance that through our deeds we influence our fates, an assurance of both our power and our responsibility. The popular representation of justice as wearing a blindfold reassures us that the power of fairness lies beyond the vested interests of individuals.

Endurance

The right metaphor can help one come up with the power needed to endure or persist despite difficulties. Runners refer to "hitting the wall" at a point where their endurance seems to give out, and to "getting a second wind." By expecting the second to follow the first, they can persist through the early strain of a race. Popular posters provide some metaphors of endurance. One says, "If life gives you lemons, make lemonade." Another shows a kitten hanging on to a rope, with the statement that "if you come to the end of your rope, tie a knot in it, and hang on." A third shows water flowing through a rock tunnel. The message of this poster is that "the best way out is always through." Remembering these simple lines with their visual metaphors, however trite, can strengthen resolve and confidence at crucial times.

Literature, like the other arts, is itself a form of cultural and personal endurance. This point is forcefully illustrated by Harlem Renaissance poet Countee Cullen in his poem "From the Dark Tower":

> The night whose sable breast relieves the stark,
> White stars is no less lovely being dark,
> And there are buds that cannot bloom at all
> In light, but crumple, piteous, and fall;
> So in the dark we hide the heart that bleeds,
> And wait, and tend our agonizing seeds.

Cullen's metaphor of darkness has multiple connotations that he celebrated rather than decried, reaffirming the worth and endurance of people whose natural darkness, rightly a form of beauty, relegates them to a social darkness in a white culture.

Mastery

When one persists through a difficult course of study, attaining competence and working toward a degree, one has gained mastery. Similarly, when one has suffered through the throes of withdrawal to rid oneself of an unhealthful habit, such as smoking, one has gained self-mastery.

Metaphors of mastery enable one to achieve a goal. To aim for the specific goal of losing weight, create the metaphor of unwanted pounds as so many potatoes in a sack or so much shortening. To quit smoking, call up the images of cigarettes as "cancer sticks" or "coffin nails." The phrase "keep a cool heart" reminds one to keep emotions in check; it can be a mastery metaphor for a person who is susceptible to the influence of others.

Philosophical Value

Metaphors with the power to encapsulate important aspects of human experience provide that special combination of insight and perspective we may call "philosophy." An example is Elbert Hubbard's epigram, "God will not look you over for medals, degrees or diplomas, but for scars." Leonardo da Vinci passed on the philosophy of his life of remarkable achievements in this metaphor: "Iron rusts from disuse; stagnant water loses its purity, and in cold weather becomes frozen; even so does inaction sap the vigors of the mind."

Metaphors that put one's own self into perspective are perhaps the most powerful of all. Alice Walker, for example, found a metaphor for herself while braiding her hair:

> As the little braids spun off in all directions but the ones I tried to encourage them to go, I discovered my hair's willfulness, so like my own! I saw that my friend hair, given its own life, had a sense of humor. I discovered I liked it.
>
> Again I stood in front of the mirror and looked at myself and laughed. My hair was one of those odd, amazing, unbelievable, stop-you-in-your-tracks creations—not unlike a zebra's stripes, an armadillo's ears, or the feet of the electric-blue-footed booby—that the universe makes for no reason other than to express its own limitless imagination. (1988, 52–53)

Through metaphor, one may devise what we can call an emotional philosophy of life. At its beginning, life is like a delicate vase, so perfect as to be translucent but also extremely fragile, whereas the determination to survive must be like cement. When life gets broken, as it inevitably does, one must rebuild it with emotional cement. The object loses its original perfection, yet it becomes stronger each time the breaking-and-mending process occurs. In time, the object may have been mended so many times that it becomes almost all cement, yet in tiny places where the original material shines through, one sees anew the beauty of the object. In the end it is the design, and not the material, that matters. What we attain through living is our own constructive activity with our lives, not an original endowment.

One may "try on" the role of another person in a difficult

position, such as the U.S. president or a high school principal, and try to reason from that person's perspective. Or one may "try on" the situation of a seabird caught in an oil spill, a Native American whose livelihood depends on game from a polluted waterway, or the captain who runs his oil tanker aground. Marriage and family counseling often involves role-playing in which members take on each other's identities. The wisdom of assuming opposing perspectives is embedded in such metaphors as "casting the first stone," "walking a mile in someone else's moccasins," and "living in glass houses."

The writer Cynthia Ozick (1986) argues that projecting oneself into someone else's situation is a form of metaphorical thinking and is necessary for civilization as we know it. According to her argument, the ancient Greeks kept slaves without projecting themselves into such a position because they could comfortably assume that *foreign* meant "subhuman." Resistance to such institutions as slavery and apartheid require people to put themselves in the place of the victims, with whom they share human status, so that they can understand that the treatment of other human beings as inferiors is not acceptable. The Golden Rule, that we should "do unto others as we would have them do unto us," is a time-honored call for this kind of empathetic metaphorical thinking. Since empathy is a necessary part of socialization and civilization, youngsters who learn its importance and practice will be more effective and civil members of society.

Trying It Out

Gaining Control through Metaphors

Through life our self-images change as we have more experiences. Today the youth of our society are deluged with experiences through expanding communications and technology. Images and ideas abound in the teenager's day, many of which mix fantasy and reality in startling ways, others of which may present subtle messages in strange disguise. The underlying messages coming from the media may be quite obvious to adult thinkers, but may escape those whose critical thinking is yet unseasoned. Michael Jackson's proclaiming that being "bad" is a good personal characteristic is a good example of the divergence between connotation and denotation. Madonna's song "Like a Virgin" implies that being *like* one is better than actually being one. Both present underlying implications that adolescents should examine.

In this lesson students are asked to examine their own metaphors for themselves with a view toward critical evaluation of both their personal self-images and those that are influential in their culture.

Activity 1   This activity centers on the terms *denotation* and *connotation*. When students can differentiate between the two types of terms, they will be ready to begin the second activity.

Write the words *female* and *male* on the board. Ask students to check the dictionary definitions of each word and any synonyms that are given. Then have them think of words that they associate with *female* and *male*. List these terms, including both words and short phrases, and do not restrict students to favorable terms only. Males, for example, may be called "man," "boy," "father," "mister," "sir," "hunk," "stud," "jock," or "gentleman." Females may be called "woman," "girl," "babe," "mother," "lady," "chick," "mother hen," or "old lady." The point of this exercise is to generate as many potential connotations for a concept as possible.

If needed, discuss the difference between the denotation and the connotation of a term. Students give their opinions of each term generated by the class and the connotations of each term. Many viewpoints will emerge, and opinions will undoubtedly differ a great deal. This not only should be accepted, but should be stressed as one of the interesting aspects of connotation.

The following questions may guide student discussion:

- What images do these connotations create in your mind?
- How does being called any of these terms affect how those listening may view you?
- How do you view yourself when someone calls you by any of these words?
- What are people revealing about themselves when they use these words?
- If we look at this list of words, do we have a complete view of what a female and male are in our culture?
- When we hear words or terms describing someone or something in a new or novel way, what are some considerations we may take into account before adding that term to our vocabulary?

    Is it in any way derogatory?

    Will it hurt someone's feelings?

    Is it a "fair" descriptor?

    What will it reveal about the person using the term?

Activity 2   In this activity students examine magazines and newspapers to find metaphors that present cultural assumptions that may influence their feelings about people and events. Bring to class enough newspapers and popular teen magazines so that each student or small group has at least one.

Ifnecessary, the class might quickly review the terms *denotation* and *connotation*. Then, working individually or in small groups, students make lists of metaphors appearing in their magazines or newspapers. Accompanying each metaphor is an analysis of denotative and connotative meaning, whether the individual or group would want to use this metaphor, and other aspects of the metaphor, such as its accuracy, effectiveness, and originality. The following questions may serve as a guide during the class discussion:

- How do newspapers and magazines influence readers by using metaphors?

- About what kinds of things can we as readers be influenced? (e.g., politics; environment; any local, national, or international issue)

- Can we be given certain ideas and attitudes subliminally if we are not attentive? How?

- How do newspapers and magazines document our national culture? Can they also help us create self-metaphors? How?

Activity 3   The third activity moves to the medium of television; specifically, commercials. Start by preparing a videotape with several teen-oriented commercials (e.g., for colas, jeans, makeup, cars). View the tape with the students and ask them to identify images in the commercials and how these images might be interpreted metaphorically. For example, a focus on a rear end in tight jeans is clearly a metaphor for sex, and a close-up of a woman applying mascara is metaphorical for personal control over one's appearance and, by implication, one's destiny. Through this activity, students can practice the notion of visual metaphors. These images can be analyzed to determine how they teach us to look at our social world and ourselves.

As follow-up, students can try the following activities:

- Create new images for products advertised on television that have clearly different connotations from the standard images.

- Plan for the "ultimate commercial" by generating the visual and textual approach that is needed to create a strong influence over the viewer.

- Write, act, direct, and produce a commercial that exemplifies cultural metaphors, videotaping this production if possible.
- Critique the cultural metaphors in the class commercials.
- Discuss the positive and negative aspects of commercials and generate ideas about how to evaluate commercials critically.

6 Extending Self to Cultural Awareness

Human beings . . . are very much at the mercy of the particular language which has become the medium of expression for their society. . . . The fact of the matter is that the "real world" is, to a large extent, unconsciously built up on the language habits of the group. . . . We see and hear and otherwise experience very largely as we do because the language habits of our community predispose certain choices of interpretation.

Edward Sapir, quoted in *Language, Thought and Reality*

Language works with experience as we develop meaning. Using language to analyze and categorize experiences allows us to evaluate their meaning and purpose and to give them a place in our whole scheme of knowledge about the world. The language that we use to describe an experience does not, therefore, merely re-create it; instead, it extends the experience, layering it with new meanings.

The concept of sacrifice, for instance, may be met at first with emotional detachment, even when we are the beneficiaries of the sacrifice. Once we have made a personal sacrifice, however, the word's connotations deepen. With each new experience, we increase our ability to sense the painful pleasure that the sacrificer feels. This is possible only because we have been there; our knowledge of the word is now filtered by our experience, and our experience has been made more meaningful by the leverage of the word.

This language-and-experience phenomenon operates in and around us, beginning in childhood and continuing throughout our lives. We label our experiences and share our metaphorical labels with younger members of the culture, who add their own perceptions as they pass them on to the next generation. Some of these metaphors become clichés—"to stab in the back," "to kiss and tell," "to cry wolf"—but we use these trite expressions anyway because we attach our own personal meanings to them.

Metaphors describe events that have happened to us or that we have seen happen to others. More striking is the endless change of language that documents the evolution of a culture's consciousness. As Mary McBride and Thomas Mullen write: "Through metaphor we create bridges, ways of crossing over from one experience to another. By analyzing metaphor, we may track the pathways of our own or another's experience" (1984, 149).

So it is with the culture as a whole. The kinds of concepts that a language does, or does not, represent in a specific word help us understand what is important in a society. Studying foreign words for which we have no equivalent is one way to do that. The Japanese have the word *zanshin*, a state of relaxed mental alertness in the face of danger, a derivative of that culture's interest in the martial arts. The Kiriwina of New Guinea have the term *mokita*, the truth about certain delicate social matters that everybody knows about, but that nobody mentions. *Dozywocie* is a Polish word meaning a contract guaranteeing elderly parents lifelong support; it is "purchased" from the children by the parents in return for an additional share of the parents' future estate. As Howard Rheingold states, "We all inherit a world view along with our native language. Untranslatable words [specific to a certain culture] help us notice the cracks between our own world view and those of others" (1988, 7).

Having a word to represent an experience perpetuates our ability to have (or at least to acknowledge) that experience. If there were no word to represent *disillusionment*, would we be as aware of the dissonance between expectation and reality? The Japanese, who have no word to represent the period of life between childhood and adulthood, have appropriated the American term *teenager*. Not having the designation meant, in effect, that no special recognition had to be given to the needs and rights of that group of people. Now some Japanese are wary as to the cultural impact that verbal recognition of adolescence (and, therefore, of adolescents) may bring.

Thus a critical aspect of metaphor as a key to cultural understanding is not merely *how* a culture represents a concept, but *whether* it represents a concept. Benjamin Whorf proposes that cultures differ in the way that they divide the natural world, organize it into concepts, and ascribe significances. The patterns do not just stare us in the face, he says. We see one pattern because of the language that we speak; someone speaking a different language is apt to see a different pattern. The Hopi word *masa'ytaka* illustrates this division of the world: while we have separate words to describe a flying insect (*dragonfly*), a flying machine (*airplane*), and a person who operates the flying machine (*flier* or *pilot*), the Hopi have just *masa'ytaka*. Whorf notes that "sometimes ill-fitting glasses will reveal queer movements in the scene as we look about, but normally we do not see the relative motion of the environment when we move; our psychic makeup is [similarly] somehow adjusted to disregard whole realms of phenomena that are so all-pervasive as to be irrelevant to our daily lives and needs" (1956, 210). Language, then, molds our thinking, our culture, and our seeing.

If we accept Whorf's hypothesis that language is an integral part of the concept of culture, what happens when we attempt to study another culture through our own language? If language is culture, might we be attempting a virtually impossible task? To filter our understanding of an alien culture through our own cultural medium, the English language, may be to invite misinterpretation and misunderstanding, a risk acknowledged in the cliché "It loses a lot in translation." Although the language barrier may not be overcome without the hard work of language study, we can try to locate and examine the metaphors that other societies use to describe their experiences and world views. We also can make an effort to understand those metaphors in their contexts, not in ours.

What would most Americans think of the Indonesian Senoi tribe, whose 12,000 members gather in groups every morning to discuss their dreams? Would they consider the members of that society to be lazy? paranoid? intuitive? or inexplicably weird? What would they think upon hearing that this fixation with dreams has been linked to the absence of violent crime and conflict in that culture? Now suppose that Americans and the Senoi both use dreams as metaphors for life. Would the metaphors be identical? Do we see dreams in the same ways?

The conventional division of philosophy into Western and Eastern thought supports the notion that our cultural environments affect and reflect the ways in which we view the world. For example, the Chinese metaphor of "within or beyond the boundary of the square" has been used for 2,000 years to differentiate between those who are concerned with physical existence (within the *fang*) and those who wander freely in heaven and earth, mindless of death and physical concerns (beyond the *fang*). As described by Willard J. Peterson (1988, 50), thinking that is within the square is based on learning through worldly artifacts. Thinking that is beyond the square relies on other-world orientation. The square itself is a metaphor for earth; the circle (beyond the square) is heaven. For those of us who are not Chinese, our ability to understand Chinese thinking rests not only upon our ability to perceive this dichotomy, but also upon our awareness of its existence.

What place does cultural awareness through metaphor have in language arts? Most English teachers would agree that transmission of cultural heritage has long been identified as a primary goal of literature instruction. Highlighting our own common metaphors and comparing them with metaphors of other languages promote multicultural awareness, as well as appreciation for the power and beauty of language. If we accept the notion of language as culture carrier, we can accept the idea that common metaphors relating to daily life and belief systems also inform us about the people who use the terms. By examining these metaphors in the context of their originating cultures, we can be led to view reality in a different way—to realize that *our* understanding of the way the world works is not the *only* explanation. Cross-cultural understanding through appreciation of metaphors, as Rheingold suggests, not only changes the way our society views the world, but also the way we interact with it.

Trying It Out

Cultural Metaphors for Death and Afterlife

The way we perceive what happens to us after we die is influenced by religious and cultural beliefs. In Christian imagery regarding death, for example, one finds symbols associated with resurrection because Christianity has taught that the dead are raised by God to live eternally. By contrast, the following explanation, recorded by Hospice chaplain Barbara Prescott-Erickson from an eight-year-old child who was in the final stages of leukemia, illustrates a life after death through the metaphor of natural transformation:

> During a walk outside, the child saw a butterfly and said, "Dying is like a butterfly. You know, like the caterpillar gets in a cocoon and goes into a deep sleep and wakes up beautiful and able to fly. That's what will happen when I die. . . . I'll wake up and be able to fly in heaven, and I won't hurt no more." (Elson 1987)

The metaphor of the butterfly's life cycle was also the basis of Ron Howard's popular movie *Cocoon*. It was praised for its sensitivity and recommended as a way for families, especially those with young children, to explain the recent or impending death of a loved one.

Knowing which images or metaphors people associate with death can help us understand more about their cultural backgrounds and their ways of viewing the world. In the following activities, students will investigate a variety of ways that humans have explained the afterlife. Invite them to examine these interpretations for both similarities and differences and then to try to name the metaphorical concept that people in that culture or religious group associate with their beliefs.

Activity 1   Students divide into groups, and each group chooses a cultural or religious group that interests them, such as the following:

African	Christian	Hindu	Native American
Buddhist	Egyptian	Islamic	Polynesian
Celtic	Germanic	Jewish	Roman
Chinese	Greek	Korean	Scandinavian

Students brainstorm possible sources of information that they might consult in order to learn how these groups do, or did, explain what happens after a person dies. Encyclopedias will probably be one of the first suggestions, but other sources may be more interesting: clergy or members of the particular group; books on comparative religion; religious books such as the *Qur'an* (Koran), *The Book of Mormon*, *The Egyptian Book of the Dead*, the Bible; magazine, newspaper, or journal articles; and films, videotapes, or other audiovisual materials. To encourage use of materials that will benefit students of different learning styles, each group might be asked to use two or three types of resources. Students record the explanations of death using direct quotes and summaries. Suggest that they note ceremonies, rituals, and symbols associated with death.

Activity 2   After completing their research, the groups can organize their material into lists of possible metaphors. Table 2 shows a sample organization of this kind of material, much of which comes from Mircea Eliade's *From Primitives to Zen: A Thematic Sourcebook in the History of Religions* (1978, 139–44, 321–422).

Such a table makes it easier for students to examine the contributions of each cultural or religious group and to look for similarities and differences in the ways that various cultures and religions view death. The following list of questions will help students with their analysis:

- Which of these cultures envisioned a world after death that is like life on earth? How many saw a world that was better or worse than earth? What do you make of those findings?

- Would you agree or disagree that some people invent comparisons between known existence (earthly life) and an unknown existence (afterlife) in order to understand that unknown existence?

- In what ways can the metaphors we use for the afterlife affect our earthly lives? (In Egypt, for example, the construction of homes was given less priority than the building of indestructible tombs. Although the ancient Egyptians were preoccupied with

Table 2
Metaphors for Death Used
by Different Cultures

Religious or Cultural Group	Imagery/Ritual/Ceremony Used at Death	Implied Metaphor
Islam	Paradise is described as "gardens underneath which rivers flow."	Heaven is a garden, a place of beauty.
	Hell contains "dwellers of the Fire [who] cry out unto the dwellers of the gardens: Pour onto us some water or some of that wherewith Allah provided you. They say: Lo! Allah hath forbidden both to unbelievers." (Sura VII, The Heights)	Hell is fire, a place of torment, pain.
	Graves must be at least six feet deep so that the dead can sit up without having their heads appear above the ground as they answer questions at the Last Judgment.	Death is like life. We retain the physical properties of our bodies.
Ancient China	Ancestor worship: The family visits graves, brings food gifts twice a year, and offers spirit money for the dead who have no family.	Death is like life. The dead have physical needs.
Early Melanesian myths	Man once shed his skin like a snake to become young again.	Life ongoing is a natural process.
Zoroastrianism (Iran)	On the fourth day after death, we may cross the Bridge of the Requiter (Cinvat Bridge) and then take the Road to Heaven or the Road to Hell.	The afterlife is a physical place to which we journey.
Winnebago Indians	One must travel to the Land of the Dead.	The afterlife is a separate spiritual realm.
Ancient Egypt	The dead were buried with food and weapons. Their bodies were preserved so that their souls (*ba*) could return to their bodies. Pictures and plaques were placed in the tomb so that each soul would find the right body.	Death is a continuation of life. The dead have physical needs for food, shelter.
	Chambers of kings were decorated to resemble their homes; many storage rooms were built—even bathrooms.	We can use our senses after death.
	The eyes and mouths of the dead were pried open before burial.	
	The hearse was boat-shaped. The life-giving Nile led to the river in the land of the dead. Kings were said to ride in the sky with the sun god, even to take his place.	Death is a journey.
	The king's heart was weighed in a balance with a feather after death. If he was not pure, he faced punishment.	Sins are heavy.

death, recent archaeological theories negate, however, the allegation that Egyptian life was relatively joyless.)

■ In what ways can these metaphors of the afterlife give us feelings either of limitation or freedom?

Explain to students that a *construct* is a framework of ideas, an understanding that is built systematically. Based on their research and discussion, how would they explain the meaning of *metaphorical construct*?

Cultural Perceptions of Time

The notion of time has great power over people's minds; our cultural assumptions about time lie deep. Westerners often feel a kind of adversarial relationship with time. We get "time on our hands" when we do not want it, but "time runs out" on us when we do. While time may "heal all wounds," it also wears on us, pressures us, ravages us, and, sooner or later, takes its toll, bears us away, and then flees.

American philosopher Henry David Thoreau characteristically had his own attitude toward time, which perhaps not surprisingly was different from most other people's: "Time is but the stream I go a-fishing in," he wrote in *Walden*. "I drink at it; but while I drink I see the sandy bottom and detect how shallow it is. Its thin current slides away, but eternity remains." (1948, 80)

Scientist Stephen W. Hawking, in his book *A Brief History of Time: From the Big Bang to Black Holes* (1988), wrote about the "arrow of time," an arrow that always shoots in a particular direction. He describes three such arrows: the psychological arrow of time, the thermodynamic arrow of time, and the cosmological arrow of time, all of which are traveling outward in the direction of the expanding universe, but whose directions could be reversed. Hawking's career has been built in part on determining the implications of this view.

In reference to the hands on an old-fashioned clock, we commonly speak of the "hands of time," which also are like unidirectional arrows, and sometimes we wish to "turn them back."

Other cultures have different conceptions of time from our own. Hindus, for example, specify the relationship between human and divine time as an exact proportion. The period from Brahma's creation to the end of the world is one divine day, or *kalpa*, equal to 12,000 years in the time of the lesser gods and 4,320,000 human years. In other words, one human year is a day in the life of the gods and a fleeting moment to Brahma (Hopkins 1971).

In contrast to Western conceptions of time as finite and

quantifiable, Eastern cultures portray images of time that emphasize fluidity and recurrence. Such images may include the flow of water, the turning of a wheel, a snake biting its tail, spirals, waves, and circles. In Christianity, too, the wreath symbolizes eternity (*Encyclopedia Britannica* 1974, vol. 17).

The Buddhist notion that all time—past, present, and future—takes place simultaneously is very difficult for the Western mind to grasp. Equally difficult to our finite way of thinking about time is the Hopi notion of duration, which excludes the notion of simultaneity (Whorf 1956, 158).

Trying It Out

Time

Following are some metaphors and clichés about time. Ask students to determine which ones they like or agree with. Most of these metaphors reflect usual human experiences. The businessperson, for example, may embrace the general notion that "time is a commodity," whereas a scholar might call for a literary work or idea to "stand the test of time." What do metaphors for time say about the culture that characteristically uses them?

> Time is a commodity:
>
> > Spending time
> >
> > Investing time
> >
> > Wasting time
> >
> > Buying time
> >
> > Borrowed time
> >
> > Time is money.
>
> Time is a living thing:
>
> > "Time, whose tooth gnaws away everything else, is powerless against truth." (Thomas Huxley, "Administrative Nihilism")
> >
> > "Time: that which every man is always trying to kill, but which ends up killing him." (Herbert Spencer, *Definitions*)
> >
> > Time waits for no one.
> >
> > Time is against us.
> >
> > Time is on our side.
> >
> > Time stood still.
> >
> > Time heals all wounds.
> >
> > Time wounds all heels.

Time is a substance:

"And, departing, leave behind us / Footsteps in the sands of time." (Henry Wadsworth Longfellow, "A Psalm of Life")

Time is a natural force:

"Time is a storm in which we are all lost." (William Carlos Williams, *Selected Essays*)

Time is a vehicle:

"Time's winged chariot" (Andrew Marvell, "To His Coy Mistress")

Time is an animal:

"There is no betrayal in the human face. / Time's fin, hoof, wing and fang struggle there." (Kenneth Patchen, *To Whom It May Concern*)

These metaphors all reflect what we might call Western perspectives on time. Other cultures have different metaphors for time. Ask students to find further examples from other cultures or to interview people from other cultures to discover their attitudes toward time. Students might also create their own metaphors for time, based on their own lives and experiences.

Examining Sociopolitical Metaphors

Extending Whorf's (1956) hypothesis that language is culture and our own hypothesis that language can be a filter affecting our understanding of other cultures, we may contemplate the ways that American life might be understood (and misunderstood) through the overseas marketing of television reruns, which themselves become metaphors for our culture. American situation comedies, medical and legal dramas, and soap operas export varying information about Americans and our way of life to people of other cultures.

Trying It Out

The Global Village

In our increasingly technological world, as Marshall McLuhan has argued, the mass media are erasing cultural differences. "The new electronic interdependence recreates the world in the image of a global village" (McLuhan and Fiore 1967, 67). The following passage from McLuhan's *War and Peace in the Global Village* suggests the degree of cultural clash that can occur. People who see the world much differently than do Westerners are forced to reorient themselves to the Western view of the world.

It's possible, even today, to encounter highly educated people who are quite unaware that only phonetically literate man lives in a "rational" or "pictorial" space that is uniform, continuous, and connected with an environmental effect of the phonetic alphabet in the sensory life of ancient Greece. This form of rational or pictorial space is an environment that results from no other form of writing, Hebraic, Arabic, or Chinese.

Now that we live in an electric environment of information coded not just in visual but in other sensory modes, it's natural that we now have new perceptions that destroy the monopoly and priority of visual space, making this older space look as bizarre as a medieval coat of arms over the door of a chemistry lab. (1968, 7)

McLuhan's metaphor of a global village implies that the people of the world are becoming an enormously large, culturally consistent group. The catalyst for this unification is the media. Cultural norms and ways of life are similarly challenged and become outmoded through the invisible penetration of electronic waves, McLuhan asserts. The global village is born as humans all over the world undergo acculturation via radio or in front of the television set.

While McLuhan supported his thesis with examples of technological intrusion into African tribal life, his metaphor has fresh applications in the 1990 and 1991 upheavals in Eastern Europe and the USSR. The Berlin Wall fell, in part, as a response to consumer demands that had been fueled by disparities of wealth demonstrated via Western television programs. Some of the first excursions East Berliners took were shopping trips to what they saw as "fairyland" West Berlin stores. Even more startling to Westerners was the plight of Romanian citizens. Their provisional government immediately abolished some of Nicolae Ceausescu's most hated policies; consumer issues were among them. The new government

ended food rationing, provided enough power to allow citizens to turn up the heat in their houses and apartments, and made it illegal to refuse medical treatment to the elderly, a policy Ceausescu had enforced to keep the population young. . . . [They] canceled food exports and took steps to improve distribution and relieve widespread shortages. . . . [Supplies] hoarded for export— and for the old communist elite—were rushed into empty stores, and shoppers were dazzled to find meat, oranges, coffee and chocolate, the kind of goods that had not been available to them for years. ("Unfinished Revolution," 1990, 30)

Activities   Students discuss Marshall McLuhan's theory that the world is becoming a global village because of universal access to the mass media. Ask them to predict the effects of "media acculturation" on norms of dress, modes of transportation and housing, and choices of food and medical products. What evidence can they cite that the media are affecting these areas already? (For example, Coca-Cola is available or at least known in remote villages, and Western-style clothing dominates some Asian markets.)

Ask students to review and share news articles relating to the political upheaval in Eastern Europe. Encourage discussion regarding the extent that consumer issues seem to have affected these revolutions.

Although Marshall McLuhan died in 1980, if he were alive today he would probably have much to say about the role of the mass media in bringing about change in Eastern Europe and the Soviet Union. Ask students to speculate on what McLuhan might say about these events, considering both the positive and negative implications of the world's becoming a "global village."

Variation   Another topic suggested by the concept of shared culture via television is the misinformation that might result through televised representations of American life. Movies such as *The Explorers* and cartoons have presented the comic situations that might result if an alien from outer space had gathered its data about humans solely from American television shows. For some of the world, however, this situation is more realistic than comedic. Reminiscent of the days before mass communication when immigrants were convinced that they would find American streets paved with gold, our news and entertainment programs have now given some foreigners an equally false, or at least incomplete, picture of the United States. A young visitor from New Zealand, who had watched many American television programs, rode down an American main street, looking at urban rot, class inequities, and bumpy streets, and exclaimed in utter shock: "America's not perfect!" The following activities will help students become more aware of how these impressions of America are formed by non-Americans.

Start by finding out the titles of American situation comedies and dramas that have been translated into other languages for foreign export. Assign students to view episodes of several of these shows and to make notes about what a foreign viewer might conclude from these shows about Americans and American lifestyles. (Encourage actual viewing of the shows. While students who rely on their memories might uncover some implications, those who view the show will probably discover more subtle implications.) A sample of the possible conclusions that students might draw from American television follows:

1. "I Love Lucy": American women are afraid of their husbands, are schemers, spend too much money, dye their hair, etc. American homes are immaculate, carefully decorated, spacious, etc. American men do not want their wives to work, treat them patronizingly.

2. "Marcus Welby, M.D.": American doctors are kind, omnipotent. Medical care is extraordinarily personal and good. Americans are rich.

3. "Facts of Life": American teens are sassy, overweight, smart, pretty, boy-crazy, girl-crazy, clothes conscious, snobby, rich, not studious, independent (little parental intervention in their lives), frivolous. Teens have it "easy." Most families can afford to send their children to private schools.

4. "Mission: Impossible": Americans can "fix" the world's problems. They are technological geniuses. They work behind the scenes through secret spy agencies. They have expensive cars, clothes, beautiful homes.

Other possibilities include "All in the Family ," "Dallas," and "The Mary Tyler Moore Show." Older shows are the ones most likely to be syndicated overseas. Encourage students to consider the effect on our image that seeing America as it was in earlier decades has for an international viewing audience.

Identify and discuss with the class those implications about American life that are favorable and those that are unfavorable. Which are realistic or true? What overall picture of American life is presented?

Ask students to decide what television program, old or new, might be the best ambassador for American culture. Which is the poorest (presenting it most unfavorably)? If students could choose one program to represent American life as it really is, what would that be? Why? Do they think most people would choose the same one? Why or why not?

Ask students to evaluate the way American life is presented via television news. Is it accurate? Is there a difference between information that is truthful and information that is representative? Explain.

Ask students to share their impressions of life in such countries as South Africa, Iraq, France, India, Mexico. Questions they might address include the following:

■ Where have you gotten your information?

■ Do you think your impression of these cultures is accurate?

- What chance is there that your view might be as incomplete or inaccurate as the views some foreigners have of America?
- How can one get a clear picture of what life in another country is like?

Arrange for a native from one of the countries you have discussed to visit the class and to share his or her impressions of daily life in that country. Be sure the visitor comments on how his or her expectations of life in the United States were or were not met. Where did the visitor gather his or her ideas about American life?

The Melting Pot

One historically popular sociopolitical metaphor is that America is the "world's melting pot," which implies that the cultures of the world unite in forming a unique meld called "America."

"Melting pot" is an expression that is so familiar to us that we may no longer think about the implications behind it. That makes it a good choice to use in introducing one of the most important critical-thinking skills we can teach our students—to examine and question the metaphors that society provides for us as ways of interpreting ourselves in relation to the rest of the world. We must ask ourselves whether the metaphor of the melting pot is logical, whether it does or does not match experiences in America, and whether the metaphor itself still is (or ever was) an accurate interpretation of American life.

Trying It Out

Looking into the Melting Pot

According to *Bartlett's Familiar Quotations*, the first use of the term "melting pot" in reference to the United States was by Israel Zangwill (1864–1926) in Act 1 of his 1908 play, *The Melting Pot*: "America is God's crucible, the great melting pot where all the races of Europe are melting and re-forming!" A picture or film clip of an industrial melting pot—such as an iron smelter—might help students visualize the central image of the metaphor.

Activities

After reading Zangwill's description, ask the class in what ways this metaphor was an appropriate one for early twentieth-century America. In what ways was it not? For example, we had many cultures in one country, but many cultural groups remained separate in their own neighborhoods. The national language was English, but other languages, especially Spanish, continued to be spoken.

Have students consider what the following historical incidents imply about the melting pot metaphor:

- Native Americans were isolated by force on reservations and removed from their lands in the 1800s.
- Attempts were made to prohibit Chinese immigrants from owning property or becoming naturalized in the late 1800s.
- A common sign at railroad offices in the mid-1800s read, "No Irish need apply."
- During World War I, our fears of Germany resulted in such persecution that people, businesses, and towns with German-sounding names often changed them.
- The Red Scare hysteria at the time of the 1917 Russian Revolution resulted in quota laws designed to prevent the spread of the communist movement to the United States.
- During World War II, citizens of Japanese descent were rounded up and interred in prison camps.

Is "melting pot" a good metaphor for the assimilation of immigrants today? To help students answer that question, have them investigate current immigration laws, the status of bilingual education, the most recent waves of immigrants and attitudes toward them, and the effects of our economic health on these attitudes.

The Statue of Liberty is a symbol for freedom to much of the world. Emma Lazarus's poem "The New Colossus," inscribed on the base of the statue, includes the lines: "Give me your tired, your poor, your huddled masses yearning to breathe free." Does this invitation conflict with our present policies? What do students think the Miss Liberty image meant to the Chinese in the 1990 uprising in Tiananmen Square?

To conclude the discussion of the melting-pot metaphor, ask students to propose alternative metaphors. Canadians, for example, speak of their cultural "mosaic." Other suggestions might be "salad bowl" or "stew."

Examining Cultural Stereotypes: White Hats

Perhaps because we have so much information bombarding us, we rely on stereotypes to help us categorize and process new events and images. They give us an image or mental pattern that allows us to take shortcuts in our interpretation of the world around us. These patterns become metaphors.

Stereotypes usually rely on shared knowledge. That's why prominent figures' names become pegs for our metaphors. In this country, for example, calling someone a "Benedict Arnold" requires no further explanation. A news commentary in which a dictator is called a "little Hitler" implies cause for alarm among readers or listeners simply because we know what the real Hitler did in the 1930s and 1940s. On the other hand, hearing someone called an "Albert Schweitzer" or a "Mother Theresa" would probably evoke positive images. Similarly, biblical and literary allusions become stereotypes when we call someone who is old a "Methuslah" or someone greedy a "Midas."

Books, movies, and television shows use stereotypical characters and plots that, if nothing else, allow the action to progress quickly because we know the formula. In other words, many of the details can be left out because we "fill them in" ourselves. The activity that follows (suggested by materials in Joseph Littell's *Coping with the Mass Media* [1972]) is designed to help students explore good-guy/bad-guy stereotyping and to determine its effects.

Trying It Out

Telling the Good Guys from the Bad Guys

Activity 1

Ask students to think about familiar characters in books, movies, and television shows, classifying them as "good" or "bad." Have them justify their assessments by identifying the characters' attributes. Develop a class list of general traits of good guys and bad guys, which might look something like the following:

Good Guys	Bad Guys
win in the end	win at first, but lose in the end
get the girl/guy, finally	do not deserve the girl/guy
assist the "underdog"	are cruel to the helpless
may or may not have money, but are happy anyway	are always looking for money (even if they already have a lot)
defend themselves	pull the first punch or gun

Conclude by discussing whether students think that most entertainment relies on stereotypes. To find out, they might try compiling a list of shows or stories that do *not* follow such a good-guy/bad-guy pattern, and they might speculate why stereotypes are used.

Activity 2

Telling the good guys from the bad was a basic survival skill in the Old West. Life was fast and hard; if we are to believe the nostalgic portrayals of those days, people shot first and asked questions later. Knowing where everyone stood could mean the difference between life and death. To relate this concept to students' lives, discuss whether there are situations today in which telling the good guys from the bad ones is vital to survival. Ask them how they make those judgments. How do they test or evaluate their judgments?

Activity 3   The following research activity will help students determine whether or not they have a tendency to rely on stereotypes in forming political attitudes and in judging the contributions of prominent people.

1. Working either individually or with a small group, students choose a historical or political figure to research. Suggest that they select someone who has a generally positive or predominantly negative image, rather than someone with a mixed reputation. (Possibilities include Idi Amin, Jimmy Carter, Fidel Castro, Catherine the Great, Shirley Chisholm, Confucius, King David of Israel, Dwight D. Eisenhower, Geraldine Ferraro, Benjamin Franklin, Mahatma or Indira Gandhi, Adolf Hitler, Saddam Hussein, Thomas Jefferson, John F. Kennedy, Ghengis Khan, Nikita Khrushchev, Vladimir Lenin, King Louis XIV, General Douglas MacArthur, Senator Joseph McCarthy, General George Patton, Ronald Reagan, Franklin D. Roosevelt, Joseph Stalin, George Washington, and William the Conqueror.)

2. Students consult library resources to compile a list of good and bad (or favorable and unfavorable) facts and deeds associated with their selected person.

3. Students' next task is to try to determine why history has judged these people as "good" or "bad" and to consider whether our judgment of them would be different if our alliances were reversed (so that we were now enemies of George Bush or allies of Muammar Gaddafi or Saddam Hussein).

4. Before each group shares its findings with the remainder of the class, compile a list of all the people being profiled. Have students mark "+" if they have a favorable impression of this person and "−" if they have a negative impression.

5. After the presentations, discuss whether most people are all good or all bad. Or, assign a journal activity based on the following questions:

   ▪ How did you feel about your original responses after hearing the groups' presentations?

   ▪ Did your opinions of any of the leaders change? Why or why not?

   ▪ In what ways can stereotypes of political leaders be helpful? In what ways can they be harmful?

- What parallels can you draw to the white-hat/black-hat dichotomy?

Activity 4   A traditional metaphor for abandoned heroes is that they have "clay feet." The use of this metaphor is generally associated with disillusionment. Ask students to analyze the characteristics of heroes that are implied in this metaphor by examining the properties of clay. Discussion questions might include the following:

- What do people expect of their heroes?
- What kinds of failures might clay feet represent?
- Name a hero (for example, a sports figure, politician, or movie star) who later fell from popularity. Why did he or she lose hero status?
- Does the fact that a hero makes mistakes erase the good that he or she may have done?

Activity 5   In using stereotypical generalizations to think about world events, we run the risk of oversimplifying complex issues. Have students think of examples of conflict in the news today or in recent history in which the United States is portrayed as a "good guy" or "bad guy." (Responses might include references to Nicaragua, World War II, acid rain, the cold war, the Iranian conflict, the Iraqi invasion of Kuwait and subsequent Gulf War, the use of world resources, the Cuban Missile Crisis, Viet Nam, Cambodia, and the U.S. invasion of Grenada.) Ask students to discuss whether the U.S. actions in these situations are or were completely good or completely bad.

To examine more than one side of an issue, ask students to pair up and to select a topic from those listed above or one of their own choosing. One student should write an argument that supports our country's response to the situation; the other student should write an argument that challenges our country's response. Next, students switch papers and discuss the arguments—not to convince one another to change the opinion expressed, but rather to understand as well as possible what the alternate viewpoint is. Students' third task is to write another argument, this time in support of that alternate viewpoint. This kind of dialectical thinking activity (Paul 1985) will demonstrate the "seeing through other eyes" that must occur in order to defuse stereotypical metaphors.

Activity 6   With the world-shaking changes going on in the Soviet Union and communist bloc countries in 1989–91, one of our traditional metaphors was challenged. The Berlin Wall, a tangible symbol of the "iron curtain" between the East and the West, fell. As a class, propose a metaphor to describe the U.S. reaction to the end of the "cold war." (Are we, for example, the band leader? the banker? an ostrich?)

Some political analysts suggest that America does not know what to do now that the USSR no longer seems to be wearing a black hat. They say that we have lost our enemy and now must redefine our own role in the world. Ask students to decide whether they agree or disagree with either of these assessments. What metaphors for future world relationships can they envision?

III Critical Aspects of Metaphorical Thinking

7 Metaphor, Language, and Thought

The comparative mind is inclined toward figurative thinking, using metaphors, models, and paradigms to explain the unknown in terms of the known.... It is creative and flexible, being capable of moving back and forth between the particular item and the whole pattern, between the facts and the variable, between data and theories, between contemplative study and other kinds of activity. In sum, the comparative mind is a particular case of the general human cognitive condition and an even more particular case of the inquiring mind.

Max A. Eckstein, "The Comparative Mind"

Our ability to think and our ability to use language are interrelated. Oral language may be the most common medium for expressing thought, but it is not the only one. Music, art, pantomime, and the written word also convey mood and meaning. As a device for labeling commonalities, language is not static. The language by which we communicate our thoughts is constantly changing. Just as cognition is more than an electrical impulse, language is more than a means of communication; it is also a tool for discovering, extending, and interpreting meaning. Language is a heuristic device.

Heuristic

The term *heuristic*, derived from the Greek verb *heuriskein*, "to find out," describes any strategy or process that leads one to intellectual discovery. Many language arts and English teachers are familiar with the use of heuristics in writing, such as brainstorming and freewriting, to generate ideas. Heuristics in learning might include concept mapping, posing and answering synthesizing questions, and discussing different perspectives. Using metaphors to teach concepts (Anderson 1986) is also a heuristic device in that the metaphor gives the concept a reality that an abstract term might not convey.

In 1947 American statesman Bernard Baruch taught the world a new concept with the metaphor "cold war," in which he captured the paradox of international hostilities carried on without battles or weapons, an especially powerful phrase after the "hot" war that had recently ended. The power of the metaphor was transferred to the concept itself, and "cold war" became part of the language for discussing postwar international relations. Like "iron curtain," "cold war" proved to be an extremely powerful heuristic, creating a mind-set that dominated world politics for over forty years.

Metaphors can be used as heuristic devices for teaching concepts in school. For example, *entropy*, the tendency of organized systems to degenerate into chaos, might be difficult to grasp as a scientific concept. But Stephen W. Hawking makes it very clear with his metaphor of a jigsaw puzzle. Suppose you have all the pieces of a puzzle in a box. While there is only one arrangement that will produce a complete picture, there is an enormous number of arrangements that will not. Hence the odds are overwhelming in favor of disorder; moreover, once you have a perfect arrangement, *any* change will increase disorder.

To teach the structure of a poem, an English teacher might use the metaphor of a chain-link fence: its structure is simple to the point, perhaps, of being unnoticeable, yet it is carefully designed to join the links in such a way that the unit gains strength from the meshing of the parts. As a heuristic to enable student writing, Huff and Kline (1987) suggest using a camera metaphor: a close-up where greater detail would be effective, a rollback where the larger structure needs to be made clear.

The idea that an electron has less "potential" energy the closer it is to the nucleus of an atom may be meaningless to a novice learner. In the following excerpt from an introductory biology textbook, the abstract concept of potential energy is made much more accessible by means of an analogy:

> A boulder on flat ground may be said to have no energy. If you change its position by pushing it up a hill, you give it potential energy. As long as it sits on the peak of the hill, the rock neither gains nor loses energy. If it rolls down the hill, however, its potential energy is released. The electron is like the boulder in that an input of energy can move it to a higher energy level—farther away from the nucleus. As long as it remains at the higher energy level, it possesses the added energy. And, just as the rock is likely to roll downhill, the electron also tends to go to its lowest possible energy level. (Curtis and Barnes 1985, 18)

Trying It Out

Song Analysis

Poetry is a rich source of metaphor, and musicians are often the poets closest to the lives of adolescents. By examining the music to which they listen, students can discover underlying metaphors. Often they hear the music in terms of a catchy beat or melody.

They listen to the notes or the chorus, but they neglect the meaning of the words. By seeing the metaphors as heuristics which lead to intellectual discovery, they can uncover hidden layers of meaning in familiar songs. Much of today's music has a message, for good or ill. By examining lyrics in search of metaphors, students can become critics of a song's worth.

Activity 1   This assignment requires careful listening to songs and the selection of one song as appropriate for analysis. Require that the song contain more than one metaphor or an extended metaphor; repetitious songs along the lines of "I Wanna Hold Your Hand" or "Shake Your Booty" are too simplistic for this kind of analysis. The song analysis can take place in two parts:

1. A brief oral presentation in which the student leads the discussion and analysis of the song

2. A written analysis to be turned in on or before the date of the oral presentation

Each student is to select a different song for analysis. Differences in critical interpretations may be discussed at the time of the oral presentation. Each student supplies the remainder of the class with copies of the lyrics. The song may be played from tape or record, or it may be performed by the student.

Suggested points to cover in the discussion and essay are the following:

- Name of author/composer, musicians, title of the song, and any other interesting and pertinent information.

- Did the singer write the song that is being performed? If not, why do you think he or she chose to perform it? Is there any background information about the writing of the song that might be helpful in understanding the author's approach or meaning?

- What is the main idea of the song? Does it contain a theme?

- Point out and explain any historical or topical references in the song.

- Identify and interpret the metaphors in the song.

- Explain the song's meaning and what it tells us. Do you agree or disagree with the author/composer? Why?

- Does the style of music or instruments played contribute anything specific to the song's message?

The following songs and performers from earlier decades yield telling metaphors for modern culture. Students are to find their own examples from contemporary music.

"The Sounds of Silence" and "Bridge over Troubled Waters" by Simon and Garfunkel

"Little Boxes" by Malvina Reynolds

"Eleanor Rigby" by the Beatles

"Brick in the Wall" by Pink Floyd

"Islands in the Stream" by Barry, Robin, and Maurice Gibb

"Sixteen Tons" by Merle Travis

"Get Off My Cloud" by Mick Jagger and Keith Richard

"Tears of a Clown" by Henry Cosby, Smokey Robinson, and Stevie Wonder

"Tie a Yellow Ribbon" by Irwin Lewis and L. Russell Brown

Paul Simon's song "The Sounds of Silence" (© 1965 by Eclectic Music Co.), for example, offers many metaphors: "A vision softly creeping left its seeds while I was sleeping . . . planted in my brain." The metaphor speaks of the growth of a dream and lets the listener know that the song is a retelling of that dream.

The "sound of silence" is an intriguing metaphor. It brings to mind the philosophical question: "If a tree falls in a forest and no one hears it, does it make any sound?" Since silence technically has no sound, what is Paul Simon trying to imply each time he uses "sounds of silence"? There is much room here to delve into the seeming contradiction throughout the song of sound and silence. Silence may have a different meaning in each verse. In the first verse silence could be the silence within the composer's mind. No one can hear another's thoughts. In subsequent verses the silence comes to represent the apathy of the people, who may be so immersed in their material, technical modern world, praying to a "neon god they made," that they remain indifferent to the plight of others.

Silence is woven into many metaphors in the song. It can be touched (second verse) and can produce an echo without sound (third verse). By repeating the incongruous idea of sound within silence, the poet/musician is jarring the listener the same way he tries to jar the "ten thousand maybe more" dream people out of their apathy and silence. The silence takes on a malevolent metaphor—growing not by the gentle creeping of a planted seed, but by the spread of a disease, cancer (fourth verse).

The image of people bowing and praying to a "neon god they made" is reminiscent of Moses' followers worshipping the golden calf, an idol that they had made. Just as Moses' people fell into lawlessness while their prophet was away receiving the Ten Commandments on Mount Sinai, so the people in Paul Simon's song need to be aroused out of their apathy by a warning. The dream people do not receive a commandment on a stone tablet; rather, their prophets write messages on "subway walls and tenement halls." Who will hear and respond to the warnings? We get the image that the poor, the homeless, and people in need will listen, those who are being ignored by others too busily wrapped up in their material, technical world. The dream people have failed to heed the author/composer as he tries to reach them with his arms, and with his words.

The song holds many more metaphors to explore. What does the metaphor of the sign represent? Since we can assume that Simon has chosen each word carefully, phrases such as "naked light" and "eyes were stabbed" need to be explored. Did Simon have the sense that he had been chosen as a prophet to relay the sign's message? What images or implications lead one toward or away from this conclusion?

It will be helpful for the class to analyze and evaluate a song in such detail before students tackle their individual pieces. Other songs that might be examined are "King of Pain" and "Wrapped around Your Finger" from the *Synchronicity* album by the Police. Sting, the lead singer who later became a soloist, had been a high school English teacher before turning rock star. His songs tend to have rich imagery and references to literature. In his album . . . *Nothing like the Sun* (A&M Records, 1987), Sting includes the songs "History Will Teach Us Nothing" and "Lazarus Heart." In discussing the latter song on the album jacket, Sting says:

> Why does tradition locate our emotional center at the heart and not somewhere in the brain? Why is the most common image in popular music the broken heart? I don't know . . . I do know that "Lazarus Heart" was a vivid nightmare that I wrote down and then fashioned into a song. A learned friend of mine informs me that it is the archetypical dream of the fisher king . . . can't I do anything original?

Activity 2   Students could also examine the visual metaphors they encounter on Music Television (MTV). Ask students to choose a particular song and to examine the differences between their own interpretations of the lyrics and those demonstrated in the video version. The following questions might aid their analysis:

- What message or attitude is conveyed?
- What visual metaphors are at play?
- Are there implications about or comparisons to sex objects, heroes/victims, slaves/masters, protectors/nurturers?

- Are the roles of men and women equal?
- Does it make a difference if it is a man or woman who is the main singer in the video?
- How do the videos present men? How do they present women?

Lateral Thinking

Closely related to the concept of heuristics is that of lateral thinking, a term made popular by Edward De Bono. De Bono (1976) tells the story of a boy who amused people by consistently taking a nickel instead of a dime when offered the choice. Always good for a laugh, this demonstration was repeated many times until at last a kindly stranger privately advised the boy that he was taking the coin that was larger in size, not in value. The boy replied that he knew that, but if he took the dime, he would never be offered the choice again.

The boy, according to De Bono, was exercising lateral thinking, the ability to perceive unconventional patterns. Lateral thinking can be contrasted with vertical thinking. A person who exercises vertical thinking is inclined to reason from the most obvious or most common explanation of a situation. A conventional boy would have preferred value to size, and the conventional interpreter thought so. A lateral thinker, however, entertains other possibilities and therefore sees a broader, different picture.

Metaphorical thinking also involves this kind of multiple-pattern perception and flexibility. It requires a broadening of perspective to reveal patterns not evident to the narrowly focused view. This broadening of perspective through conscious attention to metaphors can increase one's effectiveness in interpreting and interacting with reality.

Problem Solving

A study performed by Keith Holyoak with Mary Gick and Kyunghee Koh (reported in Rubin 1988) illustrates this point. They looked at the way medical students might use analogies to solve the problem of how to destroy an inoperable stomach tumor with radiation that was so powerful that it would also destroy surrounding tissue. Two groups of students were given different anecdotes that suggested possible analogies for solving the problem. One was an account of a battle in which a general divided up his troops to approach their target from different angles so as to cause minimum damage to the environment. The other anecdote was a description of repairing a light bulb filament by dividing a laser beam into lower intensities that converged at the point of repair and therefore avoided breaking the bulb. While only 30 percent of students who heard the first anecdote solved the medical problem, 70 percent who heard the second anecdote did so. The researchers speculated that the second comparison was more useful because of the greater likeness of surface features to the medical problem.

This observation suggests that there may be differences in analogical thinking capacity, or that some people are unaware of their ability to think metaphorically. Some students saw and made use of a comparison that escaped the notice of others. Being able to see the structural similarity between two situations with quite different surface features gave the latter students a problem-solving advantage over the others.

Reframing

The metaphorical thinkers in the example above were able to *re-frame* their perception of the problem by using another problem as a clue. Reframing is a concept much like that of Edward De Bono's lateral thinking. It suggests that people can step outside common perception and see matters in a novel way. D. N. Perkins (1981) calls this phenomenon "flexibility," implying the ability to change the shape or direction of a problem. Reframing can be usefully considered in light of schema theory, an argument that human cognition is organized into patterns of expectations that have been developed within social and cultural contexts. These schemata are usually facilitative, but can also be restrictive in perceiving problems and their solutions. Robert Marzano and his colleagues speak of a "curious paradox about schemata": whereas they are the basis of human perception and comprehension, they can also be "blinders," obstructing novel perspectives and interpretations (1988, 122).

Let us take the example of an oft-cited schema, going to a restaurant. As Americans, we have schemata or scripts for what to expect from different kinds of restaurants, ranging from fast-food places to elegant dining establishments. Will any of these schemata be useful in a situation where rice and curry are served on a banana leaf without silverware? The point of this example is that schemata are often culturally embedded and may interfere with our participation in an event outside our familiarity. If we rely on our schemata only, we thereby restrict our experience.

Cynthia Ozick (1986) links the extension of experience to metaphor in that metaphor evokes imagination, which in turn makes understanding and empathy possible. Rice and curry on a banana leaf are the south Indian version of fast food. When you finish eating, unwanted leftovers can be rolled up neatly in the leaf and thrown away. The structural similarity makes the surface differences seem less strange. That is metaphorical thinking, the ability not only to perceive novel comparisons, but to make good use of them.

Charting the Structure of Metaphors

Paul Ricoeur (1977) indicates that "the metaphor is not the enigma but the solution of the enigma." Comparing structured metaphors helps students realize how they can penetrate more deeply into similarities—or seeming similarities—between two phenomena. Structural comparisons also facilitate students' understanding of each other's views and therefore encourage dialectical reasoning, or reasoning from perspectives other than one's own.

Broad concepts lend themselves to this approach. Terms such as *happiness, school, work,* and *war,* for example, represent concepts that may be construed differently by different individuals because these concepts are relatively abstract. Because of their abstractness, in fact, they are often expressed in metaphorical language, and metaphors often include comparisons with each other.

Activities

Ask students to choose any broad term to explore. Write on the board some metaphorical phrase to complete, such as "School is _____." Then have them generate a list of words and phrases that they find appropriate for completing the metaphor, such as the following list of metaphors for school:

war	a social affair
a three-ring circus	a bore
a business	an educational sanctuary
hell	the opportunity of a lifetime
a home	a joke
a baby-sitting service	a maze
a necessity of life	a factory

Have students choose three terms from the class list, now linked via the common comparison with school, that seem clearly diverse, for example, *war, circus,* and *business.* Then ask students to generate a list of random characteristics under each of their three terms, such as the following:

War	Business	Circus
fighting	heavy competition	action all the time
survival	in-group recognition	ringmaster keeping order

has casualties	leading to "workaholism"	fun atmosphere
dominates one's life	pushes people past limits	going through paces
has a general in command	profit over people	buy your ticket, see the show, leave
no personal time	the boss is always right	watch while others perform
takes luck to survive	bonuses for the best	lots of glitz, little substance
all in the same boat	customer is always right	has star performers
it will eventually be over	always room for improvement	dangerous
heroes get medals	can get fired	wild animals

Have students draw arrows from a characteristic in one column to a corresponding characteristic in another column. An example is drawing an arrow from *ringmaster* (Circus) to *boss* (Business) or drawing an arrow from *boss* (Business) to *general* (War). Working from such a list, students set up a semantic chart that shows correspondences among the attributes of the three concepts. In the example of listing metaphors for *school*, the semantic chart might look like the following:

School	War	Business	Circus
dropouts	casualties	firings	accidents
principal	general	boss	ringmaster
grades	medals	bonuses	applause
graduation	victory	profit	top billing
social	camaraderie	status in society	party atmosphere
goof-offs	goldbrick	malingerer	?

In developing a semantic chart of correspondences, students can see how concepts converge and how they might stay distinct. The class can discuss how well the concepts really do correspond across categories. They can also consider gaps, as indicated above with the question mark, and whether these gaps may be filled in with further thought and research. As these and other charts of correspondences are developed, students can see both the possibilities and the limitations of metaphors, and they can see the fact that no given metaphor covers all the possible meanings of a concept that it partially explains. Some questions to generate from this activity include the following:

- If we had a chart connecting all of the metaphors and their attributes, would it include every part of the total concept of *school*? Why or why not?

- Why is a concept always more complex than any explanation or metaphor? (The metaphor does not duplicate the concept. Rather, it connects the concept to another so that prior knowledge may be used more effectively in achieving understanding. Concepts are multifaceted, and one cannot view all sides at once. A metaphor may give us a perspective on a concept, but other perspectives may be revealed by other metaphors.)

- What implications does this activity have for how we think about concepts?

- What implications does it have for entertaining others' views of the same concepts that perhaps differ from our own views?

8 Metaphors in Critical Reading and Thinking

The metaphor is invested with the extraordinary power of invoking multiple perspectives. By shifting the focus from the central to the peripheral limits of language, metaphors can jockey around with established categories and rule-governing procedures to allow new saliencies to arise. By dislodging us from fixed conceptual schemes, metaphors are prime for helping us place our impressions into newly fashioned units of meaning.

Paul G. Muscari, ''The Metaphor in Science and in the Science Classroom''

The Functions of Metaphor

Why do we use metaphors so commonly, and what are the powers of fresh or unusual metaphors to gain our attention, enhance our understanding, facilitate communications, and even persuade us in ways we might not expect? To be effective critical thinkers and readers, we need to understand these powers for they may have more effect on our thinking than we realize, for better or worse. A useful beginning to this development of critical awareness is Graham Low's (1988) summary of the major functions of metaphor in learning and communications:

1. To make it possible to talk about highly abstract or otherwise difficult concepts that otherwise might not be accessible to ordinary comprehension, as when musical pitch differences are described by spatial relationships, such as higher and lower pitches.

2. To demonstrate underlying connections among many different phenomena.

3. To extend thought, as when we adopt the hologram as a metaphor for the brain in contrast to, for example, a telephone network. The new metaphor provides new perspectives and can be the first step toward new knowledge.

4. To dramatize, common in many literary and political uses of metaphor, as in Buckminster Fuller's image of ''the spaceship earth'' to dramatize the demands of a closed ecological system.

5. To prevaricate, as when metaphor becomes euphemism.

6. To insulate emotionally charged subjects, as is frequently done with references to death.

7. To compress an argument.

8. To gain insights into what is not yet understood.

"Metaphor thus has the intriguing attribute," Low concludes, "of having two central but opposing roles. On the one hand it promotes greater clarity in what is said, while, on the other, it serves . . . a shielded form of discourse" (1988, 129). This dual function of metaphor—to illuminate and to obfuscate—is salient to critical thinking and reading.

Metaphors as Arguments

Metaphors are often used to present or illuminate arguments. In these cases, they can be examined structurally for the elements of argument, such as premises, warrants, and conclusions. In the following excerpt from Geraldine Woods's book *Affirmative Action*, the author uses a metaphor to argue that the history of American minorities is like an unfair race:

> It's just about time for the race to begin, and the runners are flexing muscles, reviewing strategy, and preparing for the ordeal ahead. At last, everyone is in position, and a split second later the starter's pistol goes off.
>
> But something's wrong! That black man in lane nine—his foot is caught in the starting block. And someone in the crowd is holding the arm of the woman next to him. Over there, that fellow from Puerto Rico, there's a barrier across his lane. The young Chicano, those black women—they're all caught. They can't begin!
>
> As they struggle to free themselves, the unlucky runners watch their rivals zoom around the track. One lap, two, three . . . finally all obstacles are out of the way, and the minority and female runners streak down the track, staring helplessly at the white male frontrunners, now miles in the lead.
>
> Supporters of affirmative action believe American history is something like this race. . . . According to supporters, affirmative action is not a gift to minorities and women or a punishment for white males. Instead it is simply a way of evening up the starting point of the race. (1989, 86–87)

In this metaphor, we can see that the writer begins with a *premise* that affirmative action is a good policy. Although this premise is not stated, it can be inferred from the way the argument is developed. It is important to take time to analyze the presumptive aspect of any argument, that is, to determine where the writer is "coming from"; otherwise we may be persuaded without knowing why. Because of its connotative nature, a metaphorical argument usually reveals its underlying premises quite clearly.

The *warrants*, or supporting material, of a metaphorical argument are usually the correspondences drawn within the general form of the metaphor. Here, we can see that the correspondences are primarily between different runners in the metaphorical race and the major groups that benefit from affirmative-action policies. The *conclusion* of the argument asserts that affirmative action should be viewed as a fairness measure, not as a gift.

When metaphors are used as arguments, they should be subjected to critical analysis, although such technical terms as *premise*, *warrant*, and *conclusion* may not be used. More general critical analysis of a metaphorical argument is illustrated in the following exchange between two educators, E. D. Hirsch, Jr., and Herbert Kohl. In an article explicating his ideas for improving American schools, Hirsch uses a banking metaphor to argue his point that all elementary school children should have a regularized curriculum with particular factual content:

> Children who possess broad background knowledge will be able to learn new things more readily than those who lack it. This general principle could be described, in an analogy with economics, as earning new wealth from old intellectual capital. A diligent first-grader who starts off with a dollar's worth of intellectual capital will be able to put it to work at a gain, say, of 15 percent a year. But a child who starts out with a dime's worth will not only gain less new intellectual wealth in absolute terms, but will earn even that pittance at a lower rate, say 7 percent. Why at a lower rate? Because, if we again imagine the classroom scene, we will notice that the use made of intellectual capital by deprived students is not only less extensive but also less efficient than the use made by well-informed students. (1989, 31)

In his response to this argument, Kohl points out the short-comings of the banking metaphor, at least in the way that Hirsch employs it:

> He [Hirsch] summarizes his position with a banking analogy: the facts you know are your capital, and they accrue interest in school. Facts increase the way money increases, and the more facts you start with the more facts you end with. He doesn't address the issue of whether the banking of facts leads to high intellectual performance or an idiot savant mentality, nor does he analyze the relationship of thinking skills to an informed use of facts. (1989, 50)

As this "metaphorical debate" illustrates, all metaphors construct versions of reality that, necessarily, exclude other versions. While on the one hand metaphors provide effective access to concepts and arguments, Low (1988) warns, on the other hand, that "the fact that a vehicle highlights one aspect of a topic also implies that it plays down, or hides, others." Critical examination will help us determine what implications lie outside the metaphor and whether additional information and perspectives need to be taken into account.

"Dear Editor": Metaphorical Arguments in Letters

People often use metaphors to mount the quick, incisive arguments that appear in short pieces like letters to the editor. Often it is the metaphor that will catch attention and evoke the primary response, whether positive or negative. In an interview, for example, the chair of a science department referred to one of his faculty members as a "weed" when she decided to give up her government-funded experimental research for research that investigated the effects of such research on society. He explained his metaphor by saying that a weed is a flower in the wrong environment. In a letter to the editor, a respondent criticized the metaphor, saying that the faculty member was not a weed; she had just changed from annual to perennial status.

Following are other metaphorical arguments found in letters to the editors of two Bloomington, Indiana, newspapers:

> I propose this question to the farmers of Indiana: After you have planted a field of corn, harrowed it, fertilized it, irrigated, and cared for it, would you allow it to fall to fodder in the field?
>
> How would you react if a small group of people raised the cry that harvesting corn was affecting the environment, and told your neighbors horror stories of environmental disasters brought on by farmers who did not allow their crops to go back to the soil? Or if they convinced these people that the farming industry and the workers in that industry are money-hungry rapists of the environment?
>
> This scenario is exactly what is taking place in the Northwest with the timber industry. . . . (Letter from an Oregon resident, *Herald Times*, 5 September 1990)

> If a visible object is then hidden behind something in a developing infant's view, that object no longer materially exists in the infant's mind. Let's apply this concept of the "peek-a-boo" effect to the current S&L crisis. In this case over 200 banks failed and billions of dollars were supposedly lost. Where did it all go? (Letter from a university student, *Indiana University Daily Student*, 27 July 1990)

> Lobsters can live up to 150 years, growing larger with time. They are known to mate for life, and are very intelligent, often assisting one of their fellows in trouble by taking him by the claw and leading him.

Sound incredible? Lobsters often exhibit behavior that is morally superior to many humans, yet the accepted practice is to throw them alive into boiling water.

Since lobsters are still considered a delicacy, their numbers are steadily declining, as are those of almost all wild creatures on our planet. Soon, because of the destruction of habitat, hunting and trapping of animals who are becoming more scarce, and human overpopulation, our own species will find itself in hot water more deadly than any that ever boiled a live lobster. (Letter from a local resident, *Herald Times*, 8 September 1990)

Students can analyze these arguments and can bring in other examples pertaining to national affairs or regional issues. A general discussion can center on how metaphors serve as arguments and on how far they can reach in being persuasive. In analyzing these metaphorical arguments, students may find the following questions helpful:

- What is the metaphor in this letter?
- What metaphoric form and correspondences are implied? What connotations?
- Do you agree with the premises and conclusions of the argument for which this metaphor is a vehicle?

Metaphors as Euphemisms

Metaphors are powerful indicators of both cultural attitudes and individual emotions. Death is a highly sensitive topic in any culture, and the metaphors that people devise for dealing with it reveal how they try to explain realities that are beyond their experience. This topic shows especially well how metaphors transmit cultural beliefs.

Euphemisms are words or phrases that act as verbal cosmetics for unpleasant or disturbing realities, allowing us to avoid direct language that may seem too blunt or distasteful. Derived from Greek, the word *euphemism* etymologically means "good voice"—suggesting that a euphemism somehow soothes us even though at the expense of precision. Our use of the "good voice" is especially noticeable in advertising, where skunk coats become "Alaskan sable" and used cars become "pre-owned vehicles."

In the English language there are numerous euphemisms that describe bodily functions and body parts, especially those with any association with sex and digestion. Children are taught to say "tinkle" for urinate, and people in Victorian society were expected to refer to breasts as "bosoms," even on chickens. Even medical terms may seem too blatant, reminding us too clearly, perhaps, of our corporeality when we would rather think of ourselves as creatures of the mind and spirit. Oliver W. Sacks, in his bestseller *The Man Who Mistook His Wife for a Hat: And Other Clinical Tales* (1990), referred to syphilis as "cupid's disease," and indeed even the medical term here is a euphemism, derived from the protagonist of a medieval French poem, *Syphilis sive Morbus Gallicus* ("Syphilis or 'the French disease' ").

It is not surprising, therefore, that we have many euphemisms for death. Some of these terms have an archaic sound to them, yet in times of tragedy we may still find ourselves choosing words like "passed away" or "deceased" instead of "died" or "dead."

Examining our euphemisms for death and its aftermath is a way of confronting some of our deepest cultural assumptions about the nature of human life. In the following set of lessons, students can see how euphemisms give us metaphors for understanding death as well as reflect our cultural strategies for coping with it.

Trying It Out

Our Dear Departed: Euphemisms for Death

Activity 1

As a class, students compile a list of expressions and euphemistic terms for the words *dead*, *dying*, or *death*. Working in small groups or individually, students consult some of the following materials: obituaries (if possible, some from the nineteenth century), tombstone inscriptions, thesauruses, and dictionaries. A completed list might look something like this:

1. Euphemisms for *death*

went to his reward	joined his ancestors
passed to the other side	gave up the ghost
went to Heaven	made the supreme sacrifice
was called home	cashed in her chips
passed over Jordan	went West (WWII expression)
reached the Stygian shore	pushing up daisies
met his maker	went to the last roundup
began the Great Adventure	bought the farm
fell asleep in Jesus	went to his eternal rest
was visited by the Angel of Death	stepped off
breathed her last	

2. Euphemisms for *corpse*

the dear departed	stiff
the deceased	carcass
mortal remains	

Activity 2   Ask students to look over their lists of euphemisms and to discuss the following:

- How are these expressions metaphorical?

- Describe the comparisons being made to death in each of the expressions. Which ones sound comforting? Which are scary?

- Choose a handful of the more intriguing of these metaphors. Try to determine where, when, and why the phrase originated. (Etymological dictionaries are likely sources of information. The *Oxford English Dictionary* tells when a particular word or phrase was first used.)

- Hypothesize as to what each of these euphemisms might be telling us about the user's view of death, or what picture of death is being presented by the phrase.

- What do these euphemisms tell us about our culture, both past and present? (For example, do we face death fearlessly or fearfully? with despair or hope? with anticipation, calm resignation, or dread? Which responses are more "acceptable" in our culture than others, or in specific subcultures?)

Critically Evaluating Metaphors

Jeffrey Cinnamond (1987) states that "metaphors inform and create our notions of truth, and if used frequently enough, come to a position of acceptance as the reality rather than a description of it." Awareness of metaphors can sharpen students' critical skills and make them more alert to one of the most common forms of persuasion. As vehicles for arguments, metaphors are often used to persuade or manipulate thinking. Examining "nukespeak," the terminology that bureaucrats use to euphemize nuclear war and weaponry, Edward Schiappa (1987) cites "peacekeeper" for the MX missile; "anticipatory retaliation" instead of "first strike" for dropping a bomb; and terms such as "useful life," "generations of weapons," and technological "gestation," which make weapons seem organic, if something short of human. Such language, he claims, nullifies meaning and is "designed to keep us *watching* as opposed to inviting us to *participate* in the construction of the future."

Because we use metaphorical thought so routinely, we must guard against taking the metaphorical as the literal. Commenting on the language used to define the Persian Gulf crisis in the days leading up to the war, George Lakoff (1991) examines the metaphor for war advanced by Karl von Clausewitz, a Prussian general during the First World War, that "war is politics pursued by other means." Implicit in this metaphor, Lakoff argues, is the prior metaphor that "politics is business." This set of metaphors presents war in terms of profit and loss, pitting political "gains" against financial and mortal "costs." Lakoff comments that arguments generated by this metaphorical view make war "a matter of cost-benefit analysis: defining beneficial 'objectives,' tallying the 'costs,' and deciding whether achieving the objectives is 'worth' the costs." National debate, he points out, is carried on at this level without significant questioning of the metaphors that embody the premises, that is, without questioning whether it makes sense to define war as politics and business and whether there are alternative positions that generate arguments against war.

In the same context, Lakoff examines the metonymy that the state is a "person," with neighbors, friends, and enemies and having an inherent disposition, "peaceful or aggressive, responsible or irresponsible, industrious or lazy." For such a state-person, well-being is wealth, strength is military power, and maturity is industrialization. With such personification, war can be conceptualized as a confrontation between two giants rather than the confrontation of millions of actual, flesh-and-blood people. A third metaphor commonly applied to war is that of the fairy tale, complete with villain, victim, and hero, a metaphor that seems to have proved successful. The story begins when a moral imbalance is created by the villain's offensive action. The hero then, at great effort and sacrifice that may involve crossing the sea to a dangerous place, defeats the villain and rescues the victim, whereby "the moral balance is restored. Victory is achieved. The hero, who always acts honorably, has proved his manhood and achieved glory. The sacrifice was worthwhile. The hero receives acclaim, along with the gratitude of the victim and the community."

To examine metaphors as figurative, rather than as literal, language, we need to keep in mind our own primary image, that metaphors are bridges to understanding, not to reality. Metaphors help us examine, embellish, and extend our notion of what is real, but our constant theme has been that metaphors are not to be confused with the realities that they illuminate. This is true of all language, indeed, but here we are focusing on consciously devised metaphors that offer interpretations with which we might or might not agree, or that might or might not be accurate.

Looking Closely at Metaphors

The common expression that "she eats like a bird" may be indirectly stated in a birdlike image, "she pecks at her food." In either case the imagery is not to be taken literally. Some birds actually consume ten times their own body weight in food every day. Would any 100-pound person—let alone a picky eater—really eat 1,000 pounds of food each day—approximately 4,000 McDonald hamburgers? We understand, of course, that the comparison is really between the amount a human eats and the diet of a bird. But even then, there are ostriches to consider. We need to be wary of what may be hidden inside a metaphor.

The elements alluded to in a good metaphor need to be different enough from each other to catch attention yet have a connection. In the metaphor "The boy wolfed down his food and howled for more," the elements being compared, a wolf and a human, are not the same, but the implied connection makes sense. The boy devours his food in an uncivilized way and then makes an animal sound for more. In a mixed metaphor the imagery may go awry because the connection breaks down. In his newspaper column, "The Writer's Art," James Kilpatrick quotes a city commissioner from Portland, Oregon, who wanted a gradual reduction in the number of city-owned cars: "If you try to take the whole enchilada, you get lost in the woodwork" (Bloomington [Ind.] *Herald Times*, 25 February 1990). We get lost in the metaphor because it does not sustain the connection with which it began. We start out with an image of human greed and are then disconcertingly switched over to an image of buglike disappearance.

Trying It Out

Mixed Metaphors

In his book *Anguished English: An Anthology of Accidental Assaults upon Our Language*, Richard Lederer quotes Donald Nixon, brother of the former president, as describing Watergate as a "political football [being used] to bury my brother" (1987, 76). Roland Bartel (1983), in his book on metaphor, cites Gerald Ford's statement that he prefers the long-distance runner to the short-term Band-Aid. To begin "unmixing" these metaphors, one would choose a single image to sustain, so that, for example, the "political football" might be used to score a touchdown against an opponent, or a "political spade" might be used to bury him.

Present students with a mixed metaphor, such as the following: Don King, a boxing promoter, was quoted in the January 1989 *Chicago Tribune* as saying, "Mike Tyson has come *360 degrees* around, and that's the *triangle* of life." Ask them to perform the steps listed below:

- Identify the opposing elements of the metaphor.
- What does the whole metaphor mean to suggest? In what sense are the elements "mixed"? (360 degrees equals a circle, not a triangle.)
- Rewrite the metaphor in a correct form. (Mike Tyson has come 360 degrees around, and that's the circle of life.)

Here are some further examples of mixed metaphors:

1. In President George Bush's "State of the Union Address" on 30 January 1989, he talked about democracy spreading throughout the world: a "full flowering of government which is the engine of freedom."

2. In *The Wall Street Journal*, an engineer warned against too much enthusiasm for new forms of energy: "If you get too much out of step with the mainstream, it will backfire" (quoted in Kilpatrick 1990, p. A11).

3. An Associated Press story about prospective Supreme Court Justice Douglas Ginsburg (whose nomination was withdrawn after he admitted that he had smoked marijuana) stated: "At 41 years old and a judge for less than a year, Ginsburg has left few fingerprints to provide administration critics a toehold of opposition."

Following is a list of mixed metaphors collected from various sources. Ask students to decide how they might "unmix" the metaphors. A good follow-up exercise would be to have them collect their own examples of mixed metaphors and see what unscrambling might be effective with these. Sometimes, of course, it is best just to abandon the image altogether and to start with a new one.

He came down on them like a tank and vacuumed up their objections.

The sun rising struck a death knell to her hopes of getting home on time.

He was batting one hundred on the court of life.

If wishes were horses, we would all be in the catbird seat.

Time was running out on them like steam from a kettle.

We tried to understand her, but she kept babbling nonsense like a broken machine.

If we don't all put our shoulders to the wheel, we'll be over a barrel soon.

As low man on the totem pole, he was always being led around by the nose.

Until we have some better information, we'll just have to read between the lines, keep our heads low, and play it by ear.

Trying It Out

Belabored Metaphors

Some metaphors not only have mixed elements, but they try too hard, as in this sports article in *The Los Angeles Times*:

> The Rams swore they would never forget Buffalo, and the memories of a last-minute loss there on October 16 that stuck to their insides like clumps of oatmeal, a taste so bitter it could not be duplicated, a feeling so strong it could not be tolerated.
>
> The Rams wore the wounds of that loss, a gut-wrencher of ulcer-raising proportions, like lockets around their necks, hoping it would remain close to their hearts and serve warning to a game's funny bounces and its sometimes humorless conclusions. (Quoted in "Block That Metaphor," 1990, p. 100).

This example from the *Duluth* (Minn.) *News-Tribune* earned the headline of "Most Unappetizing Metaphor of the Week" in *The New Yorker*:

> "Lawful gambling in the state is like a cancerous pizza," Bouza said. "It has enveloped the entire community, and we are the midgets who are trying to eat through the crust and the tomato sauce and bring some order to the process." (5 February 1990)

Ask students to find and bring in examples of overdone metaphors. These can be collected as "Exhausted (and Exhausting) Metaphors" on a bulletin board or in a class book.

Reverse the tables and ask students to take perfectly good metaphors and to inflate them through overwriting. Have students relate this experience to style in their own writing.

Doublespeak

A mixed metaphor often reflects the carelessness of the person who constructed it; nevertheless, metaphors in general reveal the writer's attitudes and perceptions. Metaphors can also reveal planned deception, as in doublespeak. Foreigners held in Kuwait after the Iraqi invasion were referred to as "foreign guests of host Iraq" by a spokesperson from the Iraqi Parliament and as "inconvenienced people" by President George Bush, who did not want to use the word *hostage*. *The New York Times* reported that the president was choosing his words carefully to avert the kind of hostage standoff that restricted American action in the past:

> "We've been reluctant to use the term 'hostage,' " Bush is reported

as saying. "But when Saddam Hussein specifically offers to trade the freedom of those citizens of many nations he holds against their will in return for concessions, there can be little doubt that whatever these innocent people are called, they are in fact hostages." (Rosenthal 1990)

Recognizing the maneuvering that goes on beneath the surface of such deliberately chosen words is an important first step in understanding the hidden agenda of much language and, in some cases, in defending oneself against manipulation.

The term *doublespeak* was first constructed from the words *newspeak* and *doublethink* coined by George Orwell in his novel of a negative utopia, *1984*. *Newspeak* is language used metaphorically or euphemistically to manipulate thinking or to deceive. (During the Vietnam War "air support" was used over Cambodia instead of bombs.) Orwell's term *doublethink* expresses the idea that people can hold two opposite viewpoints in their mind at the same time and accept both. (Senator Orin Hatch said in 1988: "Capital punishment is our society's recognition of the sanctity of human life" [Lutz 1989].)

Orwell was an outspoken crusader for clear language. One can use figurative language to get a point across without being deceptive, as Orwell demonstrated in his essay "Politics and the English Language" (1946): "When there is a gap between one's real and one's declared aims, one turns as it were instinctively to long words and exhausted idioms, like a cuttlefish squirting out ink." Students can gain an awareness of doublespeak by practice. If they see how deceptive language is constructed by others in examples they find, they will learn to recognize misleading metaphors.

In order to analyze doublespeak, or any metaphor, the elements of the metaphor must be understood. By their nature, metaphors are teaching devices because they compare. One may not understand an element of the metaphor at first, but if the bridge that the metaphor builds can be crossed, then the meaning may be reached.

The following criteria may be used as an aid in evaluating metaphors. Your objective as teacher is to help your students internalize the following questions as critical tools in debugging doublespeak:

- Do you think you understand the metaphor? Can you paraphrase it?

- What is the author's/speaker's viewpoint? Can you identify premises, argument, or reasoning?

- Do the elements of the metaphor make sense? Is it a mixed metaphor?

- Does the metaphor try to persuade? How?

- Is the metaphor deceptive? Does it involve doublespeak? over-embellishment? suppressing of unpleasant realities?

- What are the references in the metaphor? Are they social, historical, religious, scientific, or cultural? What previous knowledge must one have to understand the metaphor?

- Does the metaphor act heuristically, that is, lead to new ideas or understanding? What does the metaphor teach or reveal?

Through critical attention to metaphor and students' ways of evaluating metaphors, language arts and English teachers may not only find ways to enhance both creative and analytic writing, but they also may find undiscovered abilities in some students.

The analysis of metaphors is a prism through which thinking and writing encounter the creative and critical spectrum. Much as a light passes through a prism to refract the varied colors of the rainbow, using metaphors to aid expression can result in a varied mode of thinking.

Trying It Out

Exploring Doublespeak

William Lutz, editor of the *Quarterly Review of Doublespeak*, has compiled many examples of deceptive language. As students read through the following examples of doublespeak collected in Lutz's book *Doublespeak* (1989), ask them to speculate on the actual object or phenomenon alluded to in each example:

1. Erich Honecker, former chancellor of East Germany, described this object as an "anti-fascist protective rampart" (140). [Answer: Berlin Wall]

2. Supreme Court Justice William Rehnquist's physician described his patient's condition by saying that a drug "established an interrelationship with the body, such that if the drug is removed precipitously, there is a reaction" (19). [Answer: drug addiction]

3. In its budget request to Congress in 1977, the Pentagon called this object "an efficient nuclear weapon that eliminates an enemy with a minimum degree of damage to friendly territory" (15). [Answer: neutron bomb]

4. Also in 1977, a former Green Beret captain related on the Dick Cavett television show that during the Vietnam War the C.I.A. devised the phrase "eliminate with extreme prejudice" to replace this term (15). [Answer: kill]

5. Instead of a simpler phrase, the officials of the British Museum had this warning sign in the museum parking lot: "No responsibility is accepted for the safety of persons using or entering this car park or for their cars or other property, and such persons are permitted to enter and use it only on the understanding that they do so at their own risk" (147). [Answer: park at your own risk]

Activity 1

There are plenty of title-enhancement types of doublespeak in schools and in the classroom. Ask students to identify and replace the embellished educational terms below with a clearer, plainer term.

1. Learning Resources Center [library]
2. pupil station [desk]
3. classroom manager [teacher]
4. Human Movement and Leisure Study [physical education]
5. certified adolescent transportation specialist [school bus driver]

Activity 2

Ask students to look at objects around the classroom, think of subject areas, or consider any aspect of the school building. Then they are to write their own examples of doublespeak by replacing the known word or term with an enhanced version. Have them exchange their examples and try to identify the meanings of each other's embellished words or phrases.

Activity 3

Ask students to be on the lookout for doublespeak examples across the media—television, radio, newspapers, and periodicals—and to record these in a journal. One such example is a *Berry's World* cartoon in which a television announcer greets listeners: "Welcome to the morning non-fiction entertainment show. Formerly, the news" (Bloomington [Ind.] *Herald Times*, 12 March 1990).

Extended Metaphor

An extended metaphor can be a very useful figurative device, but it is important not to stretch the comparison too thin. Metaphors are most effective when used deftly and somewhat sparingly. One overworked metaphor can be the small shout in a snow-laden valley that precipitates an avalanche, so one should proceed with caution. Occasionally, however, a writer may make his or her way carefully through a long and complex metaphor and win our admiration.

Henry David Thoreau was one of the great "metaphoricians"

of our culture, and he could successfully draw out a comparison. Observe the twists and turns of the following comparison of England to a man burdened by his own materialism:

> I look upon England today as an old gentleman who is traveling with a great deal of baggage, trumpery which has accumulated from a long housekeeping, which he has not the courage to burn; great trunk, little trunk, bandbox, and bundle. Throw away the first three at least. It would surpass the powers of a well man nowadays to take up his bed and walk, and I should certainly advise a sick one to lay down his bed and run. When I have met an immigrant tottering under a bundle which contained his all,— looking like an enormous wen which had grown out of the nape of his neck,—I have pitied him, not because that was his all, but because he had all *that* to carry. If I have got to drag my trap, I will take care that it be a light one and not nip me in a vital part. But perchance it would be wisest never to put one's paw into it. (1948, 54)

Thoreau's penchant for drawing out a comparison is also illustrated in the following passage, in which he compares the formation of the human form to the development of geological phenomena:

> What is man but a mass of thawing clay? The ball of the human finger is but a drop congealed. The fingers and toes flow to their extent from the thawing mass of the body. Who knows what the human would expand and flow out to under a more general heaven? Is not the hand a spread *palm* leaf with its lobes and veins? The ear may be regarded, fancifully, as a lichen, *umbilicaria*, on the side of the head, with its lobe or drop. The lip—*labium*, from *labor* (?)—laps or lapses from the side of the cavernous mouth. The chin is a still larger drop, the confluent dripping of the face. The cheeks are a slide from the brows into the valley of the face, opposed and diffused by the cheek bones. Each rounded lobe of the vegetable leaf, too, is a thick and now loitering drop, larger or smaller; the lobes are the fingers of the leaf; and as many lobes as it has, in so many directions it tends to flow, and more heat or other genial influences would have caused it to flow yet farther. (257)

Students can find or develop their own extended metaphors or analogies, developing as many logical or fanciful correspondences as they can. These sustained metaphors can then be contrasted to the ludicrous tours de force of the exercise on belabored metaphors. Another example of a well-written extended metaphor is the chapter entitled "The Iks" in Lewis Thomas's *The Lives of a Cell* (1974), in which he compares the behavior of a maladjusted tribe to the conduct of humanity in massed situations such as large cities.

9 Metaphors and Creativity

Through metaphor, the past has the capacity to imagine us, and we it. Through metaphorical concentration, doctors can imagine what it is to be their patients. Those at the center can imagine what it is to be outside. The strong can imagine what it is to be weak. Illuminated lives can imagine the dark. Poets in their twilight can imagine the borders of stellar fire. We strangers can imagine the familiar hearts of strangers.

Cynthia Ozick, "The Moral Necessity of Metaphor"

Above all, we associate metaphors with creativity, which Timothy N. Thompson has metaphorically defined as "weaving perspectives" or "aesthetic pattern meshing." Weaving and meshing require the loosening of prior holds. "It may be necessary to disorient one's orientation before a discovery may be made," Thompson writes. To do so entails what he calls "wandering in the neutral zone," an adventure that may have some risks (1986, 1).

These notions of creativity are illustrated in the work of Bruno Schulz, a Polish writer and artist killed by the Nazis during World War II. In the following passage, he recaptures the experience of a child with crayons and paints:

> I sat on the floor. Spread out around me were my crayons and buttons of paint: godly colors, azure breathing freshness, greens straying to the limits of the possible. And when I took a red crayon in my hand, happy fanfares of crimson marched out into the world, all balconies brightened with red waving flags, and whole houses arranged themselves along streets into a triumphant lane. Processions of city firemen in cherry red uniforms paraded in brightly lighted happy streets, and gentlemen lifted their strawberry-colored bowlers in greeting. Cherry red sweetness and cherry red chirping of finches filled the air scented with lavender. (1979, 19)

Wallace Stevens is another writer who uses sensory images in evocative ways that achieve disorientation without losing balance. In his poem "The Beginning," he writes:

> But here is where she sat
> To comb her dewy hair, a touchless light,
> Perplexed by its darker iridescences. (1982, 427)

Even more illustrative of the principle of disorientation for discovery are these lines from his poem "Man and Bottle":

> The mind is the great poem of winter, the man,
> Who, to find what will suffice,
> Destroys romantic tenements
> Of rose and ice. (1982, 238)

The emotional experiences evoked by Schulz's memoirs and Stevens's poems are as sound as logic, yet they cannot be explained in the same way, and perhaps not satisfactorily by the concepts of grounding, form, correspondences, and connotation introduced in chapter 2. There is more license here and a stronger reliance on intuition, knowing not accounted for by observable processes of cognition. The hunch, the flash of insight, and the cognitive leap are often ignored in schools, where conscious, rational, and problem-solving processes receive primary attention, sometimes at the cost of imaginative pursuits. Literature, however, reserves a valid place for imagination in language arts and English classrooms, and creative literature can be written as well as read by students.

In finding their own imaginative connections between language and experience, students may find inspiration in literature that, like Schulz's passage above, deals with themes of childhood and adolescence. Consider, for example, the following passage from the novel *Anywhere but Here*, in which Mona Simpson, a late twentieth-century fiction writer, describes the experience of a child taking refuge from her mother in the bathroom:

> I pressed myself into the corner, like something molded there. I tried not to hear, not to think. And then, after, there was always a lightness, a feeling of air inside, like you are an impostor, eating only the appearance of things, living in holograms of light. (1988, 100)

One may never have had a relationship with a parent like that at the center of Simpson's novel, but one can understand a great deal through the metaphors in this passage. The child becomes a part of the wall, tries to shut down her senses, and experiences herself as an illusion. In the phrase "living in holograms of light," which conveys the disembodied feeling of aloneness, one can feel the essence of psychological neglect.

Lee Smith, a writer contemporary with Simpson, has a way of letting her characters' metaphors turn into something else, as in this passage from "The Interpretation of Dreams":

> Melanie loves how the rain sounds drumming down on the big

> skylight at the center of the mall right over The Potted Plant and
> Orange Julius. It sounds like a million horses running fast, like a
> stampede in a western movie. She loves movies, she loves Clint
> Eastwood, now what if *he* came in the outlet mall right now and
> walked over to her and said, Excuse me, ma'am, I need a king-size
> bedspread in a western decor? (1990, 129)

In the title story of Smith's *Me and My Baby View the Eclipse*, the
first premonitions of a love affair also emerge from a metaphor:

> "How's that?" He held up the drawing and Sharon said it was
> fine. Then he signed his name in tiny peaked letters across the
> bottom of it, like an electrocardiogram, which she didn't expect.
> Something about him doing this tugged at her heart. (195)

Ask students to identify their favorite metaphors in their
readings, metaphors that jarred them into seeing or thinking about
something differently. Or they may simply relate metaphors that
they found especially pleasing. Talk about metaphors that seem to
have twists, that set people off in a new direction. From this
discussion move to the question of imagination itself. How do
people extend their experiences through imagination? Can anyone
do it? Why not?

Trying It Out

Guided Fantasy: Imagining Change

Change is the essence of life. It operates in our perception and our
learning in so many ways that we often take it for granted.
Change is also the essence of metaphor and metaphorical thinking.
We engage ourselves in changes when we acquire knowledge,
when we revise, when we look at issues from perspectives not our
own, and when we discard perspectives that no longer seem useful.

Guided fantasy is a technique whereby one immerses oneself
in an idea or concept and thoroughly explores its implications and
possibilities. A famous example is Franz Kafka's story "The Meta-
morphosis," in which the main character, Gregor, wakes up one
morning and finds he has become a beetle. To begin this activity,
which was suggested by Donald Sanders and Judith Sanders (1987,
39), read aloud the beginning paragraphs of Kafka's story, in
which Gregor first realizes his condition. Then ask students to
imagine themselves waking up as someone or something else, con-
centrating on their first moments of recognition that their existence
and being have been drastically altered. The following suggestions
will help guide students into other fantasies of change:

1. Changes in nature:

   A caterpillar changing into a butterfly

   A tadpole changing into a frog

   A river changing into a waterfall (and then into a lake or sea)

2. Changes in fiction:

   Gregor changing into a beetle

   Clark Kent changing into Superman

   Lamont Cranston changing into The Shadow

3. Changes in perspective:

   How a closet looks to a cat

   How a drop of water looks to an ant

   How a train might look to a dinosaur

4. Imaginary changes:

   A pigeon changing into a peacock

   A mouse changing into a cat

   A Cadillac changing into a Volkswagen

   A Republican changing into a Democrat

   A painting changing into a song

Treat these suggestions imaginatively. They can be reversed, for example, or used simply as heuristics for students to think of their own guided fantasy changes. After students have written about changing into a different person, creature, or object, set the mood by altering the light in the room and having students read their fantasies aloud in a relaxed mood. The fantasies can also be collected into students' own "Book of Changes" or "Metamorphoses," a modern version of Ovid's classic tales.

Studies of Creativity

For a number of years, Harvard researchers Howard Gardner and David Perkins have been systematically studying the nature of creativity. Gardner believes that creativity is a culturally defined phenomenon within which individuals combine their special talents with their chosen media in order to be expressive and original. The success of the outcome, in critical terms, depends on the inter-dynamics of these three components (culture, talent, and medium). He defines creativity as "a dynamic interaction among an individual's unique blend of intellectual and personal strengths, the domains of knowledge in which those strengths are applied, and the people who judge what works and ideas are worth preserving" (Gardner and Perkins 1990, 15).

After studying creativity for twenty-two years, Perkins believes that enough is now known so that it is possible to teach people to become creative. He has constructed what he calls the "snowflake model" to suggest that every person's creativity has six components:

1. A drive to reduce complexity to order and simplicity
2. A drive to be original
3. The ability to cut across traditional boundaries and make novel connections
4. The habit of working at the edge of one's competence, pushing one's limits outward
5. Willingness to entertain criticism and different viewpoints
6. A strong need for self-direction and control over tasks

Perkins has proposed a metaphorical definition of knowledge as "designs shaped by human invention" (Gardner and Perkins 1990, 16). According to this view, knowledge is always constructed and never passively received. This view is in keeping with current beliefs in cognitive science and educational theory that emphasize the constructive, dynamic nature of knowledge in contrast to earlier, static views that tended to favor directive teaching and passive reception in learning.

If we look at Perkins's snowflake metaphor for creativity, we can see how metaphorical thinking is implicated in all six components. A metaphor can simplify a complex idea without sacrificing its meaning, as when we use the image of a spaceship to characterize the finite nature of resources and space on earth. An effective metaphor strikes us as original, as does (to this book's authors) Michael Ventura's (1988) comparison of Las Vegas to El Dorado, the mythical lost city of gold that can never really be found.

The ability to cut across traditional boundaries of thought and perceptions directly involves metaphorical thinking. The term *synectics* refers to techniques of using metaphor and analogy to take lateral steps toward novel perspectives on problems usually viewed in stereotyped ways. Metaphorical thinking stretches the mind and encourages us to take risks, or as Timothy N. Thompson (1986) puts it, to "wander in the neutral zone." At the same time, sharing metaphors exposes us to the judgments of others so that feedback is obtained, allowing us to sharpen our metaphorical skills. Finally, metaphorical thinking, because it is original, leads students toward increasing control of their own expression, fostering the self-confidence that insists on self-determination.

The Beast within Us: Finding Human Metaphors in the Animal Kingdom

In an imaginary conversation with Aesop, Willard Espy asks the great fabulist why, since his fables are intended to illuminate human nature, they almost always feature animals. Aesop replies:

> Because we think of animals as being simple-minded. . . . An animal can be used to sum up a single, uncomplicated point. My animals were clearly what they were, and said clearly what they had to say. The thoughts and activities of any human being are too complex for a quick summary. Yet the profounder the wisdom, the simpler it should be expressed. (1981, 197)

This notion suggests the intriguing possibility that we can gain a simple yet profound view of our own natures by finding the animal that provides us with our best metaphor. In fact, the psychologist William Sheldon, famous for his classification of people into endomorphs, mesomorphs, and ectomorphs, developed a taxonomy of forty-two different male body styles, each with a different animal analogue. The following excerpts typify his descriptions of extreme endomorphy (people with a predominance of digestive tissue, hence a tendency toward plumpness), mesomorphy (a predominance of muscular tissue, the macho type), and ectomorphy (a predominance of nerve tissue, the thin, intellectual type):

> **Somatotype 711**: Extreme endomorphy: A round-bodied, broad-tailed, harmless aquatic mammal who belongs to the order of sirens (*sirenia*) and is the original mermaid. He lives on aquatic plants in shallow estuaries. Out of water, almost as helpless as a jelly fish. (1954, 324)

> **Somatotype 171**: Extreme mesomorphy: Golden eagles. Cumbersome battleships of the air, as birds of prey go, yet agile enough to hunt jack rabbits with success and powerful enough to kill dogs. (64)

> **Somatotype 117**: Extreme ectomorphy: Walking sticks. Fragile, stretched-out creatures with the utmost surface exposure in proportion to mass, and therefore with maximal delicacy of structure. (36)

Since rabbits and dogs were mentioned, we might look at a couple of the "balanced" types, of which these animals represent two:

> **Somatotype 334**: Cottontail rabbits. Quiet, sensitive, introverted little herbivores who mind their business and by doing so generally manage to expand their population as fast as the carnivores can eat it up. (142).

What a difference one point in mesomorphy can make—the difference between the hunter or the prey:

Somatotype 344: Pointers. Slender, well-proportioned bird dogs, staunch on the point and sensitive to control. Eager, wide-ranging hunters, yet durable enough to stand a full day in bramble country. (156)

Sheldon's taxonomy and the descriptions he derived from it may make us wonder if he perhaps labored in the wrong field. Surely his imaginative approach to human nature would have been more appreciated in literature than in psychology. Be that as it may, his taxonomy might stimulate students to identify and elaborate their own animal metaphors, those "fables" about themselves that in a simple but profound way capture their individual characters. Sheldon's taxonomy leaves out a lot of animals. There are no primates, few birds, few rodents, and no real fish. Few domestic animals are included, and since he worked exclusively with males, his assortment of animals tends to leave out those with more feminine possibilities, such as Persian cats, butterflies, does, and swans.

Activity   As a classroom activity, ask students to write monologues, fables, reincarnation stories, or any other genre they choose from the point of view of their animals. These can be compiled into a class "Bestiary." If there is an artist in class, illustrated bestiaries are even more fun.

Other examples may also be brought to class, such as T. H. White's *The Book of Beasts* (1954), a translation of the twelfth-century Latin book *The Bestiary* or, as a modern version, John Gilgun's *Everything That Has Been Shall Be Again*: *The Reincarnation Fables*, a collection of nine monologues by animals who were once humans.

IV A Resource Section for Using Metaphors in the Classroom

10 Strategies for Metaphorical Teaching

A teacher is like a scout, who, having previously travelled the path, comes back to lead the way.

Judith Best, "Teaching Political Theory: Meaning through Metaphor"

The idea of using analogies in teaching is certainly not a new one. Educators have long used comparisons to explain unfamiliar or unseen concepts. For example, early scientists used a visible phenomenon, the movement of water in waves, to explain an "invisible" phenomenon, the movement of light and sound. We as English teachers support our students as they try to discover their own voices—a metaphorical term which helps explain that we want their writing to sound like themselves, rather than like an encyclopedia or a rhetorician. Linda Williams (1983) has listed several advantages to using metaphors as teaching devices, including the following:

1. Metaphors are more engaging than dictionary definitions because they clarify the concept as well as stimulate the mind to further exploration.

2. Metaphors present concepts in terms of students' experiences.

3. Metaphors suggest a specific context for asking questions: "If X is like Y in this way, is it also like Y in this other way?"

4. Metaphors are efficient vehicles for organizing and retaining information.

5. Teachers can assess understanding of a concept more exactly by having students generate their own metaphors.

Thinking in terms of the four aspects of metaphor introduced in the first part of this book—grounding, form, correspondences, and connotation—can help you as a teacher use this approach more effectively in at least two ways. First, you can focus on the structural soundness of comparisons. Second, you can examine the metaphors to judge the implications of accepting them as interpretations of the concepts and processes they represent. In this chapter, therefore, we focus on "metaphorical teaching," with examples of how language arts processes might be presented metaphorically.

The process of devising a teaching metaphor is both simple and complex. It requires preparation and thought; most importantly, it demands a thorough understanding of the concept. The first step is pinpointing the main idea to be grasped in a metaphorical concept. A nebulous notion may result in a fuzzy metaphor at best. The second step is generating alternative metaphors for the concept and examining not only the congruencies, but also the discrepancies between each metaphor and the concept. The examination of discrepancies will help you choose the best metaphor for your lesson. The third step is actually presenting the metaphor, allowing for ample demonstration, careful examination of both the strengths and limitations of the metaphor, and student response, which may include critiques of the metaphor or generation of original comparisons to further explicate the topic.

Using Metaphors in Teaching about the Stages of Writing

Many of the terms used in the teaching of writing are metaphorical, but because of their familiarity, they have lost their power to engage. "Composing," for example, suggests several images that involve a sophisticated combination of diverse elements for a central purpose—the arrangement of a melody or musical theme, the design of a fine painting, or even the more technical task of typesetting. Yet many of us see "compose" as simply a synonym for "write."

Language being what it is, behind every metaphor is another metaphor, and by going behind the scenes we might enrich the common metaphors upon which we tend to fall back. When we describe writing as requiring a student to "generate" ideas, we might not envision an electric plant building up steam and producing the energy capable of supplying power to writing, although such an image might be "generative" for students. When we ask students to complete a "draft," we might not evoke the image of an architect sketching a series of alternative plans, one of which might be chosen for development. We advise students to "cut" unnecessary words and phrases, but perhaps without the vivid mental pictures that go with this phrase: sharp blades releasing dead weight to save a sinking ship or to relieve the burden on a poor peddler's back.

Our traditional metaphors may have lost their provocative power, but we can invigorate old terms with new images or make up new metaphors for complex processes, such as writing, that will help our students think through what they are doing.

Metaphors for the Writing Process

Activity 1

Devise and present an extended metaphor for the writing process or use the one provided below:

Writing as Weaving: Writing is like weaving. In weaving, we select the yarn, sorting among many colors and weights. These colors and weights might represent the elements of setting, mood, theme, plot, and character that we will entwine. If these elements come from our own experiences, we may compare ourselves to the weavers who grow, cut, and spin their own flax into yarn and then dye the skeins different colors.

Deciding to make a sweater, scarf, or afghan out of the yarn can be compared to developing an idea as a story, poem, or essay. Perhaps we have a product in mind and even a definite pattern as we start to write. Or perhaps, like some weavers, we will let the texture and the colors of the yarn lead us into what we will produce.

Like weavers, we must physically entwine the threads of our stories. Otherwise, the plot will not hold together. Mistakes in the weaving process result in flaws in the fabric. Flaws may weaken the design both of cloth and of stories, or they may add the touch of idiosyncracy that marks the piece as an original. The Japanese have a word for this phenomenon, *wabi*, the flawed detail that sets off an elegant whole (Rheingold 1988). For the most part, however, we will probably consider flaws as structural mistakes that we do not want to leave in.

To create a design, we must make every circumstance, every action, connect with one another. As we weave, the pattern becomes more and more apparent. After each row of the warp is interlaced by the weft, the threads must be pushed together tightly, just as a writer does in revising a story. The construction of a good story is as tight as that of a good piece of cloth. We even speak of plots as being interwoven and of stories as being tightly meshed.

Editing a story is like looking for the disruptive flaws in the cloth, so that we can unravel and reweave any problem areas. When we are satisfied with the piece, the time has come for us to take it off the loom for our own enjoyment and to offer it to the public for admiration and, perhaps, purchase. Weavers sell or give their products away, just as storytellers perform for the pleasure of their audiences and writers write to be published.

Discuss with the class how the comparison between writing and weaving succeeds, as well as how the metaphor fails. For example, students might point out that weaving is different from writing in significant ways. Weaving usually requires a plan that cannot be changed once the piece has been started. Removing mistakes is extremely painstaking work, so it is better to move carefully and get it right the first time, to avoid unraveling and reweaving. This is quite the opposite of the advice that we give to writers; we tell them to get *something* down on paper and then to rework, rewrite, review, reject, and revise. The weaving metaphor falls short, then, because it does not capture the fluidity and recursiveness of the writing process; nor does it specifically address the possibility of revisions of all kinds at any stage.

Nevertheless, the weaving metaphor is productive in helping students understand important aspects of writing, especially in emphasizing its originating, imaginative aspects. The point is that students will learn more from examining both the relevant aspects and the shortcomings of the metaphor, and this may encourage them to continue the search for an even better metaphor to describe their experiences.

Activity 2   Examine metaphors that professional writers use for describing their processes. Such metaphors, gathered by Barbara Tomlinson (1986; 1988), compare writing to gardening, hunting, fishing, cooking, sculpting, painting, sewing, and tailoring, and compare revising to tying things off, repairing, and cutting. These comparisons of writing to familiar and physical tasks help students view writing less as a mysterious art for which one must have a special gift and more as the hard work and deliberate craft that it is. One example from Tomlinson's collection, ''writing as mining,'' especially emphasizes the drudgery involved:

> *Writing as Mining*: Some authors compare their writing to prospecting; ideas are out there—albeit scarce and concealed—a writer just has to *find* them. As James Dickey implies, a writer isn't necessarily any more talented than the next guy; he just keeps at it. Creative genius isn't essential: ''No matter how back-breaking the shoveling is and running it through the sluices and whatever you have to do to refine low-grade ore, you have the dubious consolation that what you get out of it is just as much real gold as it would be if you were just going around picking up nuggets off the ground.'' (1986, 61)
>
> Ideas, then, are resources—hard to obtain, inherently valuable, but in need of processing. As Tomlinson notes, writers must follow the vein wherever it leads, digging until the deposit is exhausted. Low-grade ores have to be refined to make them valuable, just as an author's inspiration has to be polished to make it publishable. (More than one writer has applied Edison's definition of genius in saying that good writing is 1 percent inspiration and 99 percent perspiration.) Prospectors and writers alike may search a long time

without discovering the mother lode, but sometimes they uncover a rich vein unexpectedly.

Activity 3   Help students develop other metaphors. Divide the class into groups and ask each group to develop a metaphor for writing as a process by comparing it to treasure hunting, house building, moviemaking, navigation, space exploration, or any of Tomlinson's suggestions. Encourage students to come up with their own ideas as well. By devising writing metaphors, students can strengthen their understanding of writing and perhaps gain insight into aspects of their processes that need revamping. Metaphors increase metacognitive thinking and, therefore, student involvement in learning.

Various stages of the writing process suggest a range of metaphoric possibility:

Prewriting: percolating, simmering, flashing back, focusing, browsing, housecleaning, blueprint making, mapmaking or map reading, taking inventory of stock on hand

Writing/drafting/composing: pouring a foundation and putting up stud walls, beginning a journey, sewing a garment together, panning and zooming in with a camera

Revising and rewriting: throwing out the first batch, fine focusing, cropping the original picture, tuning the car or a piano, applying paint and wallpaper, redecorating or changing color schemes

Editing: pulling a few weeds, smoothing the icing, reprinting the picture with a gloss finish instead of a matte finish, straightening one's clothing and adding accessories, healing the wounds left by cutting

Publishing: holding an open house, attending opening night at the theater, sharing pictures from your trip with neighbors

Trying It Out

Metaphors That Help in Teaching Self-Editing

Many metaphoric mini-lesson topics can be developed to teach self-editing strategies. We have labeled each syntax problem below with grammar terminology, but use of the terms themselves is not essential (nor advisable) in demonstrating techniques that students can use to improve their writing. What is important is to equip students with tools for editing their own work and that of their peers. We think the imagery of metaphor helps to do that.

Activities

1. Dangling Modifier

"S. Florida illegal aliens cut in half by new law." (*Daily Iowan*, 3 March 1987) [Ouch! What a sharp piece of legislation!]

Slowly sinking in the west, we watched the sun go down in a splendor of colors. (Were we standing in a swamp or just falling off the edge of the earth?)

"Dangling modifier" contains its own metaphor. The idea of a group of words hanging on, half-connected to the sentence, is a humorous image to most students. You can develop the metaphor more fully by adding detail. For example, the modifier might be described as a person hanging onto a cliff or the ledge of a building. The modifier must find the word that it describes, so it inches along the ledge (the sentence), checking each word it passes to see if it can get a toehold, that is, to see if it "fits." Unfortunately, sometimes the word that the modifier describes cannot be found on the ledge at all; it is still inside the building (the writer's mind), looking out the window!

Drawing pictures of ludicrous examples of dangling modifiers can further show the absurdity of the construction, as shown in the figures accompanying the following sentences:

1. While walking toward the stage, his face turned red. *Better*: As Homer walked toward the stage, his face turned red.

2. Blocked from kicking, the ball made its way into the end zone anyway. *Better*: Blocked from kicking, the quarterback carried the ball into the end zone anyway.

3. Butterflies may become extinct by using pestidices. *Better*: Our overuse of pesticides has endangered all species of butterflies.

Challenge students to find and illustrate their own examples of dangling modifiers.

2. Misplaced Modifiers

Here is a picture of my dog which I have placed in this envelope. (Is this cruelty to animals, or is it just a very big envelope?) *Better*: In this envelope is a picture of my dog; or, I have placed a picture of my dog in this envelope.

Remember the old cartoon in which the mouse family receives a kitten from the stork? Just like the misplaced modifier, the kitten belongs *somewhere*, but not *there*. Mrs. Mouse kept her misdeliv-

Figure 1
Walking face.

Figure 2
Self-propelled ball.

Figure 3
Butterfly working spray bottle.

ered bundle, but we writers want to relieve our sentences of their misplaced descriptors.

Collecting such bloopers from spoken and written language will make an entertaining bulletin board display. The daily newspaper is a good source to check, as these examples cited in the *Columbia Journalism Review* show:

> "The following bipartisian [sic] members of Congress will meet with the President at 9:30 this morning on Competitiveness in the Cabinet Room." (White House press release, 24 February 1987) [Can't they get along anywhere?]

> "Officials to monitor games for mosquitoes." (Lafayette [Ind.] *Journal and Courier*, 15 May 1987) [What kinds of games do mosquitoes like to play?]

> "City Orders Four Police Dogs to Rebuild Corps." (*Williamsport* [Penn.] *Sun-Gazette*, 23 July 1986) [And what if the dogs refuse to rebuild the corps?]

> "Infant abducted from hospital safe." (Ashland [Ky.] *Daily Independent*, 6 February 1990) [What was the infant doing in the safe in the first place?]

3. Nonparallel Construction

Sentences that do not use parallel construction may be wordy and unclear, but may not appear "ungrammatical." Students therefore often need help in recognizing when and how to use groups of words with similar or corresponding structures, as these examples illustrate:

> The dealership advertised an inventory-reduction sale for this weekend and is promoting a manufacturer's rebate. [*Better*: This weekend the dealership is advertising an inventory-reduction sale and is promoting a manufacturer's rebate.]

> Biking is a favorite hobby of this track star, who also likes to camp equally well. [*Better*: This track star's favorite hobbies are biking and camping.]

To explain this editing strategy, ask students to think of synchronized swimming or chorus-line dancing: the swimmers and dancers, all of whom are different from one another in appearance, mirror one another's movements to effect a balanced and pleasing impression. The rhythmic representation of phrases or clauses as sound patterns helps to develop students' abilities to hear problems in nonparallel construction.

4. Lack of Agreement

Lack of agreement can be a problem both within sentences and between them. Even competent writers occasionally switch from one pronoun to another or from one verb tense to another; the self-editor needs to be able to spot these slippages.

Not all offending passages are as confusing as the classic

Abbott and Costello routine, "Who's on First?" but any switching of person or tense within a piece can be annoying to a reader. As one aim of a writer is to communicate, careless shifts must be eliminated:

> Every*one* should pay *their* taxes on time. If *he* doesn't, the rest of us suffer. [*Better*: Everybody should pay their taxes on time. If they don't, the rest of us suffer.]

Confusion can also be a result of inattention to a pronoun's antecedent, as in this example from a small-town newspaper:

> "Recent visitors were Eli E. M. . . . and their son-in-law Jacob H. . . . Jacob had his tonsils removed in Hanover. It was a pleasant surprise to have them for supper." (Sugar Creek [Ohio] *Budget*, 2 March 1990)

Prepare yourself for a whole-class groan after students hear that one.

5. Run-on Sentence and Sentence Fragment

"Calvin Klein was released from a New York hospital after a six-day stay for injuries his horse dropped on him." (*San Jose* [Calif.] *Mercury News*, 11 July 1990)

Most run-on sentences do not make as much sense as this one does, with its unfortunate double meaning. The run-on sentence is a metaphor that evokes images of words tailgating or rear-ending and becoming jammed together in heavy traffic. Everyone has experienced the frustration of not being able to get a word in edgewise. Written run-ons have a similar effect on readers, who wish they could get some punctuation in edgewise.

To demonstrate the fragment metaphorically, you might use the example of a torn, partial message:

> In the last box on the shelf . . .
>
> Wherever the key could fit . . .
>
> Because the jewel is under the stone . . .

Each example contains only a fragment of a sentence—perhaps a partial clue to a treasure. Sometimes clue-readers will be successful in finding the treasure, sometimes not—which accurately represents what happens to readers of sentence fragments. Sometimes they can guess the intended meaning correctly; sometimes they cannot. And sometimes this truncation of meaning is a desired literary effect and is stylistically acceptable.

6. Clarity   Additional examples of problems in clarity follow; we might use this catchall category for all syntax problems, including those described above.

A metaphor for clean style is the sparkling water of a brook. It flows quickly, splashing and alive. We can easily "see to the bottom." Muddy style, on the other hand, is full of the silt of a sluggish stream. Its murkiness discourages potential readers. In revising and editing our writing, one task is to filter out the silt. The purified stream then becomes palatable for others.

Ask students to "filter" the following sentences and phrases to eliminate problems in clarity. A variety of errors are represented here, including a few spelling bloopers that changed the intended meaning. (All were cited in "The Lower Case" column of the *Columbia Journalism Review*.)

> "Rock star hit with sick child." (*Mansfield* [Ohio] *News Journal*, 4 August 1987)
>
> "Runaway truck misses family." (*Somerset* [N.J.] *Spectator*, 1 October 1987)
>
> "Akron balks at paying flat fee to recycle energy plant advisor." (Akron [Ohio] *Beacon Journal*, 9 December 1987)
>
> "Fire Suspected as Arson Guts Three Haddam Structures." (*Middletown* [Conn.] *Press*, 13 March 1986)
>
> "Medical Ethics are the choices we make based on our value system or moral considerations in the field of medicine. The symposium will help people develop principles to make decisions. One example is youth in Asia. You have got the choice of letting a person live on a machine or pulling the plug. What's right?" (Brookings [S.D.] *South Dakota State University Collegian*, 5 March 1986)
>
> "Millerton students join against drinking while drunk." (North Canaan [Conn.] *State Line Free Press*, 21 June 1986)
>
> "Low-Rise Building Aims at Serving Smaller Tenants." (*Los Angeles Times*, 20 July 1986)
>
> "Police kill man with TV tuner." (Oceanside [Calif.] *Blade-Tribune*, 3 June 1986)
>
> "Owners Responsible for Biting Canines." (*New Albany* [Ind.] *Tribune*, 9 September 1985)
>
> "ServiceMaster Keeps Schools Cleaner; Helps Control Infections, Head Lice, Teachers, Custodians, Others Claim." (Elkins [W.V.] *Inter-Mountain*, 21 October 1985)
>
> "Dishonesty policy voted in by Senate." (*Ball State* [Ind.] *Daily News*, 8 February 1985)

"Singapore addicts turn to dried dung." (*San Francisco Examiner*, 11 May 1985)

"Man minus ear waives hearing." (*Jackson* [Tenn.] *Sun*, 26 May 1985)

"U. S. Grant to Help Clear Lake Weeds." (*Burlington* [Vt.] *Free Press*, 18 May 1985)

"Another body found missing." (Gainesville [Fla.] *Sun*, 21 June 1990)

"State police hang flier in search for a suspect." (*Hartford* [Md.] *County Sun*, 7 October 1990)

"Flu Escalates to Epidemic Stage; Kills Most People in Eight Years." (Ithaca [N.Y.] *Cornell Daily Sun*, 26 January 1990)

"Hafen is an enthusiastic reader and claims 'Lame is Rob' by Victor Hugo as her favorite book." (Rexburg [Idaho] *Scroll*, 4 April 1990)

11 Metaphors That Help in Teaching Reading

Reading books in one's youth is like looking at the moon through a crevice; reading books in middle age is like looking at the moon in one's courtyard; and reading books in old age is like looking at the moon on an open terrace. This is because the depth of benefits of reading varies in proportion to the depth of one's own experience.

Chang Ch'ao, quoted in Rudolph Flesch,
The Book of Unusual Quotations

Descriptions of the reading process can be powerful tools for increasing students' confidence, interest, and ability. Unfortunately, the wrong metaphors can likewise undermine confidence, erode interest, and thwart ability. For example, the general metaphor of reading as "inquiry" has the potential to encourage readers to be active researchers into their own questions, but the metaphor of reading as "absorbing" may saddle readers with a perception of failure when they do not sense themselves automatically filling up with knowledge. We need to become aware of the usually unconscious assumptions behind some metaphors that superficially seem useful.

A Sample Metaphor for Reading

To demonstrate the importance of analyzing the metaphors that we use as heuristics in the classroom, consider the metaphor, presented in one study skills text, that reading a paragraph is like opening a can or jar of food. The metaphor suggests that the paragraph is a container and the meaning is the nutritional and possibly perishable goods within. There are many kinds of food containers, of course, and as many ways of getting them open: one can twist, tear, punch, pull, peel, or use tools. Some containers may yield easily, while others may resist and require a stronger hand or special measures. Sometimes we may abandon the effort, and other times we may want to smash our way in, perhaps destroying the contents in the process. The variations on this metaphor seem endless, but does that make it a useful metaphor? Underlying this metaphor are implications that fly in the face of current reading theory and practice.

Examining the Metaphor

This metaphor, which evokes a strong mental image of readers wrestling with cans of words, may not be a helpful or accurate view of the processes that good readers use. The first problem teachers will encounter in using this metaphor is that it fails to differentiate between efferent and aesthetic reading. The metaphor implies that all reading is efferent—and that readers, therefore, are on a fact hunt when they read. Efferent reading has been described as "reading [in which] the reader's attention is not focussed on the experience with the text but with the 'residue' or the information to be sifted from the text" (Prest and Prest 1988, 128).

If we apply this metaphor purely to efferent reading, we can emphasize the challenge of digging in to "get the can open." The work involved in comprehension is applicable both to poor readers and to skilled readers. One of the drawbacks of the metaphor, however, is in the implication that getting the can open is more than difficult; it is, in fact, impossible unless you have the right tool, the "secret." This message may not be the best to build students' confidence as they tackle arduous reading tasks. Moreover, it may encourage the misconception that there are study skills "tricks" that can alleviate the readers' work in understanding.

Instead, we need to make students aware that most readers do not analyze the types of paragraphs they are reading in order to decode the message. Rather, they plunge right into their reading, backing up when necessary to reread. If they choose to tackle a problem paragraph, they may ask someone else to read it and to explain the author's intent, or they may go to a dictionary for assistance. More often than not, however, they will just skip over difficult passages that confuse them, relying on the subsequent paragraphs to give them more information. Good readers try to maintain momentum as they read, and while they employ effective strategies, their attention is on the meaning of what they read, not on the strategies themselves.

Applying this metaphor to aesthetic reading (Rosenblatt 1938; Rosenblatt 1978), which is reading as an experience rather than reading as a means to another end, stymies us even more. If we assert that all of the meaning in a passage is "in there," in the can or text, we discount what the reader brings to the text. In aesthetic reading, readers bring their own feelings and experiences to what they read. They associate what they are reading with their own lives. They do not assume, as the above metaphor does, that all the meaning is on the page. Teachers can help students have confidence in their own interpretations by giving them opportunities to work through and discuss their own responses, and by showing that all texts have multiple interpretations.

Alternate Metaphors for Reading

1. "Aim for the Block"

Annie Dillard uses a kindling-splitting metaphor to describe her own writing process. Like many writing metaphors, this one is equally applicable to reading:

> At first, in the good old days, I did not know how to split wood. I set a chunk of alder on the chopping block and harassed it, at enormous exertion, into tiny wedges that flew all over the sandflat and lost themselves. What I did was less like splitting wood than chipping flints. After a few whacks my alder chunk still stood serene and unmoved, its base untouched, its tip a thorn. . . .
>
> One night . . . I had a dream in which I was given to understand, by the powers that be, how to split wood. You aim, said the dream—of course!—at the chopping block. It is true. You aim at the chopping block, not at the wood; then you split the wood, instead of chipping it. You cannot do the job cleanly unless you treat the wood as the transparent means to an end, by aiming past it. (1989, 42–43)

What Dillard learned about meaning is that it is beyond the individual word. "There is another way of saying this. Aim for the chopping block. If you aim for the wood, you will have nothing. Aim past the wood, aim through the wood; aim for the chopping block" (1989, 59).

2. "Warm Up and Cool Down"

Like someone who begins a running program after years of not exercising, the student encountering a new level of academic challenge may find that the muscles require some work to get into analytical shape. The muscles that are not in shape really hurt when they are worked the first few times. So too with the brain. There are times when thinking abstractly is easy. There are other times when abstract thinking requires entirely too much effort. With the pain, however, comes strength. The following metaphor comes from the reader response journal of Shevawn Eaton, of the Learning Skills Center at Indiana University:

> When discussing various reading skills in class, I talk about skimming a chapter as a mental warm-up to focus the brain's energy and attention onto the task at hand. I refer to the summary as a "cool down," a way to bring all the muscles into line, examine them, assess the weak areas, and condition them for the next run."

3. "Look through a Magnifying Glass"

Students should be expected to form opinions about what they have read—to decide whether they like or dislike, believe or reject, the information. Students must be made aware that even though a reading is nonfiction, they should not assume it is therefore all factual. Students sometimes accept anything in print as true, not realizing that authors are often trying to persuade readers, even in informational writing, by what they do and do not include. Persuasion aside, every piece of writing conceived by a human mind features a point of view.

A magnifying-glass metaphor might be devised to help students alert themselves to look for the subtext in anything they read. Even textbooks have a "hidden agenda," all the more hidden insofar as they purport to be unbiased; the agenda is evident in what they do and do not include and how they deal with controversial issues.

4. "Read the Map and Follow the Signs"

Using map and road analogies, you can help students learn to "follow the signs" provided by titles, headings, subheadings, boldface type, chapter previews and summaries, learning objectives, discussion questions, glossaries, footnotes, and indexes. A footnote, for example, can be compared to a historical marker—not vital to one's arrival at a specific destination, but of interest and perhaps worth the delay to examine. Chapter previews, on the other hand, are like stop signs; readers need to pause and think before proceeding. They might spend this time predicting what they will read and considering what they already know about the topic.

5. "Chart Your Own Route"

As an extension of the map metaphor, a comparison between readers and car drivers might focus on the importance of drivers' maintaining control of their cars and their destinations. The authors may have a plan in mind that they want us as readers to follow, but we have the power to accept or reject the roads they wish us to take.

6. "Don't Think about It—Just Ski"

In their classic text on reading, *How to Read a Book*, Mortimer J. Adler and Charles Van Doren have provided some of our most memorable metaphors for reading, including the following comparison with skiing:

> When done well, when done by an expert, both reading and skiing are graceful, harmonious activities. When done by a beginner, both are awkward, frustrating and slow.
>
> The point about skiing, of course, is that you should not be thinking about these separate acts that, together, make a smooth turn or series of linked turns—instead, you should merely be looking ahead of you down the hill, anticipating bumps and other skiers. . . . In other words, you must learn to forget the separate acts in order to perform all of them, and indeed any of them, well.
>
> It is the same with reading. Probably you have been reading for a long time . . . , and starting to learn all over again can be humiliating. But it is just as true of reading as it is of skiing that you cannot coalesce a lot of different acts into one complex, har-

monious performance until you become expert at each of them. (1972, 55–56)

7. "Pigeonhole" and "X-ray"

Adler and Van Doren also speak of "pigeonholing" a book before reading, that is, discovering its genre or other category, and "X-raying," that is, reading the book with "X-ray" eyes to find subsurface meanings. "Every book has a skeleton hidden between its covers," they write. "Your job as a reader is to find it" (75).

8. Metaphors Based on Theory

As teachers, we ourselves draw upon one or several metaphors in conceptualizing the reading process. We need to examine these for their implications and to see if they are consistent (or need to be). For example, Dillard's "cut through the block" metaphor might seem similar to Adler and Van Doren's "skiing" metaphor, but on inspection we realize that the "skiing" metaphor is advocating much more of a separate skills conception than the "block" metaphor. The metaphorical nature of our interpretation of a complex process is evident in the concepts and models that have guided prominent reading and comprehension theory, as shown in the following metaphors.

Reading as decoding. This metaphor is associated with translation and communications theory. Reading involves translating from an aural to a visual symbolic system. The metaphor implies espionage operations, such as cracking codes and revealing hidden meanings.

Reading as transaction. This metaphor is associated with commerce. Reading involves a two-way bargaining between reading and text. Each brings something to the other and receives something back. The metaphor implies that in a successful transaction, both parties feel they have gained.

Reading as interaction. Associated with chemistry, this metaphor differs from the transaction metaphor in implying a kind of spontaneous outcome from the joining of two elements. One implication of the metaphor is that the resulting "compound" can still be analyzed into its constituent parts.

Script theory. This metaphor obviously comes from theater and drama. It implies that we learn how to act in particular scenarios of life and bring this knowledge to bear in comprehending a text. We expect various "roles" to fit together and compose a "plot" that makes sense.

Schema theory. This metaphor may be associated with architecture or any field emphasizing design. A descendant of Gestalt theory, the belief that the human mind constantly strives to construct meaningful patterns, the schema metaphor implies that we construct basic plans or blueprints that we elaborate or alter with new information.

It is well worth the time for us as teachers to think through our metaphors for reading. We can also learn more about our students by inviting them to construct their own metaphors and to examine each other's. There is no good reason to insist on a single metaphor. A useful repertoire of metaphors for different reading occasions may be the most useful "tool kit" for students striving to be versatile users of print.

Trying It Out

A Metaphor for Reading Fiction

Activities

Students make an inkblot picture, using blank paper and colored ink or paint. They squeeze or splatter some of the ink on the paper and then fold the paper, spreading the ink between the two halves. When they open the paper, they will see a symmetrical design.

Introduce the metaphor of "reading as inkblot" by reading aloud the following paragraphs, or devise your own description.

> Reading a poem or story is a little like looking at an inkblot. Perhaps you have used inkblots in a game or seen Rorschach inkblots in a psychology book. The interesting facet of the inkblot test is that people see all sorts of images and designs in the inkblot, and people differ from each other in what they see.
>
> So we can compare reading and inkblot interpretation. Just like an inkblot, a poem's or story's words are physically on the page, but how you interpret the content, organization, and tone or mood of both inkblots and literature depends on the emotional and intellectual experiences you bring to the picture or story. In other words, your feelings, your experiences, and your prior knowledge affect your understanding. They help determine the meaning you find. That meaning may differ from someone else's, or even from your own at some other time. You may like or dislike a piece, find it funny or sad, happy or disturbing. You can find it similar to your own experiences or strikingly different. You are the judge.
>
> That does not mean that you cannot benefit from hearing others' responses, of course. Usually you will find possibilities that you had not thought of and that will enrich your view of the piece. Once someone else has expressed a new meaning, you may suddenly be able to focus differently on that piece of writing and to see something new in it.
>
> Something that did not make sense to you may suddenly be meaningful because of the experiences or feelings that someone else has shared. Realizing that there are multiple meanings also can provide you with a strategy for handling passages that you thought you did not understand. Imagine looking at that passage just as you would an inkblot—from different angles, upside down, and so on. Perhaps a change in perspective is all you need for it to make sense.

Discuss with the class what the metaphor implies about the nature of reading and how it may be criticized. Sample student responses may include the following:

- The reader controls his or her own reading process.
- The reader's experiences make an important contribution to comprehension.
- The reader's response to the piece is of prime importance.
- There is no right or wrong way to think or feel about the writing.
- Looking at a passage from a different point of view or angle can help it make sense.

Students might use any one of these five implications about reading as a response question for an in-class or independent reading selection.

Encourage students to discuss the limitations of the metaphor. The following questions might help guide the discussion:

- How is a work of art not like an inkblot?
- What is the difference between a purposefully created work and a randomly created design?
- How does responding to an inkblot differ from responding to literature?

Ask students to write in their journals about their own reading strategies. Have them consider what positive and negative assumptions they have held about reading and interpreting what they have read. What new attitudes would they like to adopt? What old ones will they drop?

12 Importance of Metaphors across Content Areas

Metaphors cultivate the mind. They prepare furrows for planting ideas, which in time grow to mature understanding. If the climate is too arid for learning or if work has been neglected for too long, metaphors can break through an unreceptive crust to more fertile ground where the nutrients of teaching can be absorbed.

Howard A. Peele, "Computer Metaphors:
Approaches to Computer Literacy for Educators"

The appropriate uses of metaphors and the ways we critique them differ across content areas. Metaphors are more likely to be used as arguments and models in social science, as disposable heuristics in science, as imaginative truth in literature, and as learning aids in process instruction, from reading and writing to problem solving. Fostering students' ability to recognize, critique, and use metaphors is appropriate in all areas and can begin in elementary school.

Metaphors engage us in a deliberate effort to override the literal in favor of the imaginative; the mind is at play, involved in pretending, which is the imaginary transformation of objects and people into something else. Linda Gibson Geller (1984) suggests that elementary teachers can structure situations to elicit metaphorical thinking, such as having children emulate something that they can be "as quiet as" while passing through halls. Class discussions on such questions as "What is a shell?" elicited first graders' comparison of shells to other things, such as their ears or small dishes. Questions like "What is the difference between a turtle shell and a sea shell?" lead students to compare, find likenesses, and make distinctions.

John Barrell and Wendy Oxman (1984) describe a procedure for fostering secondary students' ability to use metaphors. Their strategy includes (1) exploring the meaning of metaphors in everyday use, (2) analyzing formal metaphors from different subject areas, (3) exploring metaphors for increasingly abstract concepts, (4) devising metaphors for subject-related concepts, and (5) evaluating metaphors through discussion. This instruction, they found, enhanced students' learning and critical thinking skills.

In her English classes, Hildy Miller (1987) teaches students to analyze metaphors in a variety of contexts, both literary and non-literary, ranging from one-liners to metaphors diffused through long passages. Students work on examples in class, speculating on the possible meanings of the metaphors, why the authors chose to use them, and their effects on readers; then students work on other passages independently. Finally, they choose a concept to develop via metaphor in a brief essay. Through this combination of collaboration, individual work, and writing, students become sensitized to the widespread use of metaphor, its varied purposes, and its conceptual power.

In social studies, Wayne Mahood (1984) recommends teaching students to use metaphors as models or schemata to build understanding, letting the imagery of the concrete (e.g., Baruch's "cold war") serve as a lens through which to conceptualize the abstract. Judith Best (1984) illustrates this principle in an anecdote she uses to teach the principle of division of power. When she and her brother were children, her father handled disputes over a shared bottle of soda by allowing one child to pour the beverage into two glasses and having the other take the first choice. The power of distributing the soda was given to one child, while the power of choosing the fullest glass, should the distribution be unequal, was given to the other.

Metaphors can function in much the same way in science. For example, one science textbook, to make clear the smallness of the nucleus in relation to the rest of the atom, compared it to a bee in a football stadium. Such metaphors serve an organizing function, according to Paul G. Muscari (1988), so that facts that appear to the novice as infinite in number and fragmentary in meaning can be viewed as functional in relation to a familiar conception of the world. At the same time, Muscari emphasizes that metaphors work heuristically in science, but they do not serve as representations of fact. They are useful to aid conceptualization or to stimulate insight in the construction of knowledge, but they should be discarded in the expression of the meaning of that knowledge. For example, all the metaphors for the atom, from the plum pudding to the orbital models, have been effective heuristically in pursuing knowledge about the atom, but they do not accurately represent the atom's structure. A facetious version of this point is a Gary Larsen "Far Side" cartoon showing a scientist madly scribbling equations on a blackboard. The caption reads, "Einstein discovers that time really is money." As soon as you take a metaphor literally, it becomes a joke.

Once we realize the pervasiveness of metaphor in all subject areas as well as in all areas of life, we begin to appreciate its importance in the language arts class. While virtually all instruction is language based, it is the English or language arts teacher's mission to focus on skill and sensitivity in language use. By helping students develop their metaphorical thinking, we are empowering them as learners across all subject areas.

Trying It Out

Metaphors to Aid Learning in Science

Another use of metaphor is to help us focus on important issues or processes through imagery. As part of the introduction of a concept, you can find or devise metaphors that help illustrate it, and then help students analyze the ways the metaphor does and does not work.

Activity 1

Students listen to or read the following descriptions and then guess the concepts that are portrayed:

> . . . not an enormous void, but more like a boundless, flexible sheet that can be stretched and squeezed, straightened and bent. All forms of matter—from pinheads to planets—create indentations in it, bending it around themselves. (Yaukey 1990) [Answer: space]

> Imagine, for example, placing a bowling ball in the center of a trampoline, and then rolling a marble around the perimeter of the sagging canvas mat. Eventually the marble will roll down the indentation of the mat into the bowling ball, just as eventually the Earth will spin into the Sun. (1990) [Answer: gravity]

Then show how the two metaphors can be tied together. As Yaukey explains, the "sheet" of space can be shaken to generate "gravity waves":

> Extending this concept Einstein believed that space can be shaken by the objects that move about in it. Gravity waves caused by an exploding star would be analogous to the vibrations of the trampoline caused by dropping a bowling ball into it.
> These waves would not be undulating through space, but slight warps in space itself, expanding and contracting anything they encounter. They would be detectable only by the way they change, ever so slightly, the shape and size of everything they pass through. (1990)

Discuss with students how the two metaphors, and the way that the author combined the metaphors, helped them understand a concept that might otherwise be quite difficult to grasp.

Activity 2 Ask students to choose a concept from any subject they are taking and to explain it using one or more metaphors. You might recommend that they should first learn as much about the topic as possible and consider different ways to define it. Then they will have the grounding to devise a metaphor or set of related metaphors to explain the chosen concept. Small groups of students can work together to devise metaphorical explanations or to critique each other's metaphors. After this initial feedback, students can share their metaphors with the whole class, perhaps using a guessing-game format.

Activity 3 Not only do metaphors help students learn about science concepts, but they also help scientists in discovering scientific precepts. Robert R. Hoffman (1980) writes, "As the incompletenesses of a metaphor are disclosed, the metaphor can be modified, perhaps to the point of generating a literal hypothesis." Have students read and discuss the following passages. What new metaphors can they imagine to advance their further understanding of the brain? of other topics?

> **The Heart:** Indeed, as Jonathan Miller (1978) argues, the function of the heart became clear only after the invention of the pump. Indeed . . . the function of the heart became knowable only after the invention of the pump. Once people understood how a pump worked, they could use that knowledge to make sense of the heart's function. With the advance of technology an analogy was provided which enabled understanding of things which were otherwise quite mysterious. (Egan 1986, 31)

> **The Brain:** We have no adequate mechanical analogs of the brain. We have seen constant attempts to make sense of it in terms of increasingly sophisticated technology. The earliest analogs were natural. Late medieval textbooks represent the brain as a kind of tree with knowledge categorized in various ways as leaves or branches from a trunk representing, often, theology. Later it is represented in terms of clockwork. Then, with a better understanding of the mechanics of the body, we find the brain represented as made up of parts that functioned like muscles—leading to faculty psychology. In this view, the parts, or faculties, of the brain grew and remained limber through exercise, much as a muscle does.
> Once the telephone and then telephone exchanges were built, we find those providing an analogy for thinking about the brain. This was considered especially appropriate as it was discovered that there was also some kind of electrical activity going on in the brain itself. It seems fair to say that behaviorism, as an overall theory about human behavior, owes more to the telephone exchange than it does to observations of behavior. . . . (31–32)

At this point, you might direct your students' attention to the most recent machine metaphor for the human brain, the computer, and ask them to discuss its implications. Following that discussion, they can read Egan's interpretation of this metaphor:

> The computer allows us, analogically, to think about brain functioning in a more sophisticated way than does the telephone exchange. The computer tends thereby to destroy the basis of behaviorism. But it is itself, of course, merely a relatively simple machine, and so provides us still with mechanistic analogies for thinking about the brain. (32)

Are there other possible metaphors for the brain that are not mechanistic? One that has been suggested is the hologram. Students might explore the implications of that metaphor and how it differs from those already discussed. A further activity might be to find other metaphors for the brain or other complex processes.

Activity 4   Metaphors sometimes obscure rather than enlighten, as the following passage on the "movement" of atomic "particles" shows. Why do you think the "false" metaphor persists? Does it serve a useful purpose despite its "falseness?"

> Let me focus on the property called "spin." At the level of description in physical theory "particles" are not masses. They do not spin. But then, why use the word "spin," and where did its use arise? Spin *is* a proper word used to describe the angular momentum of particles. Spin does not refer to motion as in a spinning top. Nothing actually rotates, or speeds up or slows down, for that matter. The property is fundamental to the particle—change the spin and the particle has changed. Beams of particles can be magnetized, accelerated, collimated, and otherwise separated out into bunches of pure types. Observations show that some particles break up into two photons. One is labeled a "spin-up" photon, the other is labeled a "spin-down" photon. Otherwise, they are alike in the math. If it seems confusing, that is because it is. An elementary particle in quantum mechanics is not even a particle in the sense of being a spatially extended body. In this case, metaphorical language persists despite its falseness. (Hoffman 1980, 400–401)

Is "falseness" the correct word to use here? Will the further discovery of information provide "literal" language that is better than the metaphors used now?

Understanding the Atom

Choosing just one metaphor is not always the best way to help students understand a concept. In dealing with especially complex topics, it may be advisable to start with a relatively simple metaphor, analyze its applicability, and then introduce successively more appropriate (and more complex) metaphors. This process of defining the concept through evaluation of metaphors is supported by research on cognition and learning. Comprehension of a new idea depends on knowing what it is not, as well as what it is.

Activity

Give each student a Tootsie Roll Pop (which will transform the class into one of the quietest classes ever). State that this candy shares a feature with the structure of the atom. Having students generate ideas should bring out the concept of the dense central part of the structure of the Tootsie Roll Pop and of an atom. Through discussion or lecture, lead to analyzing how the comparison falls down—specifically, that an atom's "outer shell" is not solid.

Using a dandelion gone to seed, demonstrate that the nucleus of an atom is surrounded by an electron cloud. Determine the weaknesses in this comparison: electrons are not stationary; they orbit the nucleus.

Ask the class to generate metaphors that take into account the fact that electrons move. Someone is likely to mention the solar system as a model. One disadvantage of this metaphor is that it is not tangible in the same sense that the earlier two examples are. The concreteness of the earlier ones, however, has helped to build student understanding and has allowed them to layer increasingly complex characteristics in order to visualize the invisible atom.

Using Metaphors to Understand Social Studies Concepts

Teachers of any subject can help students become aware of the masking ability of metaphors discussed in "Critically Evaluating Metaphors" in chapter 8. By realizing the potential of language to affect us, we control the metaphor rather than letting the metaphor control us. This principle is especially important in social studies.

Readings on national and world affairs are replete with metaphors. As sociopolitical metaphors can have persuasive purposes and hidden implications, we include social science metaphors for examination in this lesson.

Activity 1   Discuss with your students the metaphors in each of these foreign relations terms:

Open-door policy (1900): the opening of Chinese ports to the rest of the world, promoted by U.S. Secretary of State John Hay.

Big-stick diplomacy (ca. 1904): "Walk softly and carry a big stick" was President Theodore Roosevelt's metaphor for the U.S. policy of influencing other countries through business investments.

World's police officer: post–World War II America's view of its international role of "keeping the world safe for democracy."

Doormat diplomacy: some political analysts' view of current U.S. foreign policy, implying that the United States has its welcome mat out and opens its doors. An alternate interpretation of the same metaphor might be that it allows itself to be stepped on by other nations. Students might discuss both these connotations.

The following questions may help guide the discussion:

- How do you react to these metaphors? Do they evoke positive or negative images for you? Explain.

- In what ways are the metaphors accurate descriptions of our relationships with other countries for the times in which they were used? In what ways are they not accurate? What value do they have in helping us look at history? at current events? What disadvantages do they have?

- What metaphors could you think of or devise to describe any foreign policies implemented by the United States in the last twenty-five years?

Further discussion may center on current or recent events on the world scene. Questions such as the following may stimulate thinking:

- Was the Vietnam War the end of the police-officer role for the United States? What does our presence in the Middle East imply? What might be other metaphors to guide U.S. foreign policy?

- What are the implications of calling U.S. citizens held in Iraq "hostages"? How might that term, as opposed to "detainees," affect policy decisions and the attitude of the public toward them?

- What metaphor should we now use for relationships between the United States and the Soviet Union, now that "cold war" is no longer appropriate?

Activity 2   Discuss the mental pictures evoked by the following economic terms. Look for current terms in business publications to increase this list.

Stock market crash: the 1929 "fall" of the Dow-Jones index led to "smashed" hopes, "broken" dreams, "ruined" lives, and the Depression. What about the more recent "crash" of 1987?

"Prosperity is just around the corner": President Franklin D. Roosevelt's metaphor for how soon America would return to normalcy was intended to evoke belief in "happy days," an antithesis to the "depression days."

New Deal: FDR's metaphor for the programs that he was instituting to improve the economy told people that the game was changing. If they did not like the "cards" they had been dealt, they could have a "new deal."

Inflation: in contrast to depression, inflation refers to "ballooning" costs and wages.

To understand the power that these metaphors conveyed when they were first used, students should consult with relatives and neighbors who lived during the thirties and forties.

- Ask your relatives or neighbors about their feelings toward these terms. Invite them to reminisce about those years and about other slogans that they may recall. Ask them about their attitude toward President Roosevelt and his policies and why they think he was reelected three times.

- What power do slogans have over people's emotions and intellects? Prepare a presentation on the power of slogans by using examples from today's newspapers, television programs, and other media.

Activity 3   War is another area in which metaphors are prevalent. Ask students to discuss the following metaphors and other military terms (see also the Doublespeak lesson in chapter 8):

Carpetbaggers: post–Civil War opportunists who attempted to fill their suitcases (carpetbags) with Reconstruction money.

Reconstruction: both the physical rebuilding of the South and the restructuring of the entire society, its politics, and its economy.

Hawks and doves: those who were for and against the Vietnam War (also known as *warmongers* and *peaceniks*). A new metaphor arising during the Iraqi invasion of Kuwait is "owl." What is an "owl's" attitude toward war?

Home front: comparison of nonmilitary effort to contribution of soldiers that was popularized in World War II, implying that war efforts at home were as important as those on the battlefield.

Loose lips sink ships: World War II slogan warning military personnel and others not to divulge any information, however trivial, concerning U.S. military activities.

Further discussion might focus on the following questions:

- What are your reactions to these metaphors? Do they evoke positive or negative images?
- What are the implications of each metaphor?
- What kinds of metaphors come to mind for the kinds of military and political conflicts we are having today—in Latin America, in the Persian Gulf, and in America's relationships with Libya, Lebanon, South Africa, the USSR, and China?

Activity 4   Ask each student to choose another social term that invites metaphorical thinking. After researching to find out how and when the term was first used, students prepare a short talk on the term, sharing background information and explaining the imagery behind the metaphor. Suggestions include the following:

muckrakers	pocket veto
Teapot Dome	olive-branch petition
mushroom cloud	gag rule
spoils system	bandwagon
gold fever	checks and balances
domino theory	Underground Railroad

A look through your social studies textbook might suggest other terms based on metaphor. For current metaphors, look on newspaper editorial pages and at news headlines.

V Conclusion and References

Conclusion

T hrough this book we have attempted to capture some of the intellectual and imaginative possibilities that metaphorical thinking has to offer. We have enjoyed and tried to share the humor, the cleverness, and the poetry of metaphors. We have explored the power of metaphors over our images of ourselves and others; we have looked at how metaphors are involved in our cultural awareness; and we have examined the power that an unexamined metaphor may have over our political and social spheres. We have found how metaphor reveals culture and can be a means for gaining broader cultural awareness, and we have come to appreciate the importance of metaphor in getting us to think dialectically rather than judgmentally, not only for seeing another point of view, but for seeing *from* that point of view. In short, we have become convinced, truly, that metaphor plays a powerful and essential role in virtually all thinking and learning.

We began this work with a scholarly notion of research, searching out metaphors and discussions of metaphors in documents and literature, but soon our interest in this library-based research gave way to a greater interest in the library itself, not as a place of books, but as a place of people.

Here, in live transactions through talking, writing, and learning, we found metaphors abounded, and we began to listen more attentively to our contemporaries as well as to those whose words had been canonized from earlier times. We carried this attentiveness with us wherever we went, listening to the metaphors that we heard in conversations, in classrooms, in the media, at home, and in our own personal attempts at understanding. We got our students and colleagues to join the search, and soon we were bringing together all kinds of books, articles, contemporary literature, song lyrics, cartoons. Virtually anything that conveyed meaning by language or images, which is to say anything used in human communication, yielded the kind of material we sought, and in such abundance that we were overwhelmed.

A biology teacher likened the amount of ice on the earth to ten ice cubes—nine cubes would be the amount of ice in Antarctica, with one cube representing the ice in the rest of the world. A columnist called politicians the "Waring Blenders," the "Cuisinarts" of mixed metaphors. A third-world writer compared technology to genetic material, saying that it reproduces the culture that produced it, and calling for caution in the adoption of Western science by developing countries. A math teacher compared the concept of zero to the desk of an absent child, pointing that it held a place for her whether or not she was present.

Another way to look at the magnitude of our subject is to ask this question: What is left of the balcony scene in *Romeo and Juliet* if one removes all the metaphors? One is left with nothing. This exercise could be repeated with any image-rich writing and then continued with other, more prosaic pieces. As one delves deeper into the language and truly excises every metaphor, one will be left with virtually nothing except maybe a few articles and other structure words.

Finally, we reached the obvious conclusion that, because there is so much more to be shared on this subject than our small book could accommodate, we can never stop. And so we are continuing to collect metaphors and to relate them to teaching, and as our conclusion here we would like to ask *you* to leave *us* with a metaphor. What is your metaphor for the student-teacher relationship? Or a favorite metaphor you use in teaching, in learning, or in any aspect of your life? Please send these metaphors to the authors in care of the Language Education Department, Indiana University, Bloomington, IN 47405, and we will get on with our next project of compiling these into a reference for teachers. One thing we have learned from our present study: there is always another bridge to cross.

A Selected and Annotated Bibliography of Books on Metaphor and Language

The English language is a widely explored topic in both academic and popular writing. Thanks to its "impurity," English includes terms (and their etymological stories) from virtually every culture of the world. Through borrowings, coinings, and metaphorical extensions of meanings, English has developed the largest vocabulary of all languages in the world. While some might wish that English would conserve itself more and remain more consistent and fastidious over time, we personally applaud the risk-taking, globe-trotting nature of our language and hope that it will continue in this "lifestyle" indefinitely.

But, of course, these are not characteristics inherent in the language. They reflect the attitudes of people who have used it, attitudes of openness and inventiveness rather than protectiveness of the language in a given prestigious state. It is we, the speakers of English in all of its manifestations around the world, who foster the versatility and adaptability of the language. The following selected subset of books on the history, etymology, and semantics of English represents the endless fascination that writers have had with the language and the many resources available to the teacher who believes that fostering language awareness and imaginativeness are important in the teaching of English.

American Heritage Dictionary Editors. 1987. *Word Mysteries and Histories: From Quiche to Humble Pie*. Boston: Houghton Mifflin.

> This dictionary tells, in narrative style, the stories behind common English words that standard dictionaries do not include. Many of these words have metaphorical backgrounds, such as *paparazzi* (the swarming, persistent photographers of the rich and famous, whose appellation comes from the Italian word for mosquito) and *fizzle* (as in "fizzle out," which once meant, literally, "to break wind without making noise").

Asimov, Isaac. 1969. *Words of Science and the History behind Them*. New York: New American Library.

———. 1972. *More Words of Science*. Boston: Houghton Mifflin.

These books represent strata of word history in the field of science, with the second volume building on the first to reflect the increase in scientific terms during the ensuing period. Words treated range from simple terms, such as *cell, oil,* and *line,* to unusual words, like *archeozoic* and *elasmobranchii*. Words are discussed in informative essays, which include the history and etymology of the terms. Asimov has written many other word books, including *Words from Myths, Words in Genesis, Words on the Map, Words from Exodus,* and *Words from History*.

Bartel, Roland. 1983. *Metaphors and Symbols: Forays into Language*. Urbana, Ill.: National Council of Teachers of English.

The author's stated purpose for this book is to increase student appreciation for metaphor and to show the universal human liking for uncommon comparisons. Working with a very simple definition of metaphor as "any comparison that cannot be taken literally," he reviews metaphors in riddles, folk expressions, proverbs, clichés, slang, and literary sources. Defining *symbol* as "any sign that has acquired extra meaning," he explores the importance of symbols in human thought and expression. The book provides a rich, readable background for teaching metaphor and symbol.

Bernstein, Theodore M. 1988. *Bernstein's Reverse Dictionary*. New York: Random House.

This book enables the reader to find the intended word by looking up its meaning. In this way it may be helpful in reducing a long phrase to a single term if one is seeking conciseness.

Byrne, Josefa Heifetz. 1974. *Mrs. Byrne's Dictionary of Unusual, Obscure, and Preposterous Words: Gathered from Numerous and Diverse Authoritative Sources*. Secaucus, N.J.: University Books.

The author claims that this book contains a selection of the "weirdest" words in the English language. Although no information beyond brief definitions is given, readers may be tempted to pursue further research on such words as *hunkerousness* (opposition to progress), *Bletonism* (the ability to perceive an underground water supply), and *savate* (fighting with the feet).

Chapman, Robert L., ed. 1986. *New Dictionary of American Slang*. New York: Harper and Row. Revised edition of *Dictionary of American Slang*, edited by Harold Wentworth and Stuart Berg Flexner. 1975. New York: Thomas Y. Crowell.

With some 25,000 entries, this book is considered the definitive dictionary of slang. It contains expressions reflecting the most recent social developments as well as a list of suffixes commonly used to coin new terms, which might inspire students to make their own additions to American slang.

Claiborne, Robert. 1988. *Loose Cannons and Red Herrings: A Book of Lost Metaphors*. New York: W. W. Norton.

Claiborne's dictionary of lost metaphors is an entertaining collection of words and phrases whose original literal meanings "have been obscured or erased by time and change." He shares his fascination with the lore of words and engages the reader with what he calls the hidden poetry behind lost and "mislaid" metaphors. If you have ever wondered why Yankee Doodle called the feather in his cap "macaroni," you will find that it concerns not pasta but vanity, a reference to the dapper members of London's Italy-loving Macaroni Club. Being a "fall guy" refers, rather gruesomely, to being the passenger thrown down from a sleigh to occupy the wolves while others rode away to safety.

Dickson, Paul. 1990. *What Do You Call a Person from. . . ? A Dictionary of Place Name Derivatives*. New York: Facts on File.

Why are people from Cedar Rapids called "Bunnies?" The name reflects a play on words: "See der Rabbits." As we expected, one of the longest and most comical entries listed some of the many explanations for the word *Hoosier* (an Indiana resident), including the story of Dan Quayle's attempt to present a nonbinding resolution to change the definition from "botch a job" to "someone who is smart, resourceful, skillful, a winner, unique and brilliant." A step-by-step account is given of the demise of that resolution. For name-droppers, this book is a must.

Green, Jonathon. 1984. *Newspeak: A Dictionary of Jargon*. Boston: Routledge and Kegan Paul.

Using Orwell's own words, this book is devoted to that "medium of expression . . . to make all other modes of thought impossible." Examples of this kind of jargon include *injection*, referring to the process of sending a satellite or manned capsule into orbit, and the well-known *Peter Principle*, coined by Canadian educator Lawrence J. Peter, who stated that in a large organization an individual rises to one level above his or her actual competence. There will be other entries that may surprise the reader, for example, the real meaning of *legs* in the movies.

———. 1987. *Dictionary of Jargon*. Boston: Routledge and Kegan Paul.

Despite 21,000 entries covering the jargon of a wide range of occupations, the author disclaims that this is a comprehensive dictionary. It is nevertheless an impressive inventory of special vocabularies that have developed in such fields as printing, custom cars, advertising, finance, sailing, commerce, economics, boxing, business, mountaineering, gliding, computing, weaving, cattle raising, politics, basketball, railways, car sales, and many, many more.

Lakoff, George, and Johnson, Mark. 1980. *Metaphors We Live By*. Chicago: University of Chicago Press.

Perhaps the most influential book on metaphor to date, Lakoff and Johnson's work establishes the bold proposition that "all human thoughts are metaphorical." In an analysis of how metaphors operate so pervasively in language and thought, they define the functioning of metaphors and explain many aspects, such as structural metaphors, which focus the mind on certain features of phenomena, and orientational metaphors, which reveal particular cultural and personal values of users. Their discussion culminates with a statement regarding the relativistic nature of communications: that it should always be viewed in terms of negotiation rather than exact exchange of meanings.

Lederer, Richard. 1987. *Anguished English*: *An Anthology of Accidental Assaults upon Our Language*. Charleston, S.C.: Wyrick.

Lederer has done an interesting kind of research here, gathering a large collection of bloopers, malapropisms, mixed metaphors, and grammatical accidents that will bring comic relief to the longest of English-teaching days. Besides student writing, he takes on journalism, advertising, and politics. His final piece, an exposition on "American Slurvian," will erase whatever doubts that the language perfectionist might have that English is collapsing in on itself. As examples he cites *torment*, a competition, as in "Mabel and I entered a bridge torment," and *mince*, a unit of 60 seconds, as in "I'll be back in a few mince."

———. 1989. *Crazy English*: *The Ultimate Joy Ride through Our Language*. New York: Simon and Schuster.

Determined to have fun, Lederer takes an exuberant romp through the "paradoxes and vagaries" of English, to which he ascribes a "unique lunacy" among languages. With relish he turns up oxymorons, doublespeak, sesquipedalianisms, deceptive spellings, and, of course, widespread proliferation of meanings for words due in part to the metaphorical fertility of the language. An outstanding feature of the book is a dialogue of several pages in which one character (Doctor Rotcod) speaks only in palindromes, but manages, more or less, to make sense. Not only will readers of this book believe that English is crazy, but they will also realize that they knew it all along.

Long, Thomas Hill, ed. 1980. *Longman Dictionary of English Idioms*. London: Longman.

A traditional lexicon of standard British idiom, this dictionary will fascinate American readers who, despite being native speakers of English, have never heard many of the expressions. Such entries as "cloud cuckoo land," "the curate's egg," and "keep in cotton wool wrap," though common enough in the United Kingdom, may have a fresh ring on this side of the Atlantic.

Lutz, William. 1989. *Doublespeak: From "Revenue Enhancement" to "Terminal Living": How Government, Business Advertisers and Others Use Language to Deceive You*. New York: Harper and Row.

The detailed subtitle of this book is a brief abstract of its contents. Contained within are rich examples of deceptive metaphors, including sections on how educators use doublespeak, which should make all educators sit up and take notice. Lutz's information is designed to empower the reader by raising sensitivity to deceptive uses of language and by honing critical reading skills.

McCrum, Robert, William Cran, and Robert MacNeil. 1986. *The Story of English*. New York: Viking Penguin.

This book, written to accompany the PBS television series that is now available to teachers on videotape, explores the astonishing reach and diversity of the major world language, which now has more second-language speakers than native speakers. The many ramifications of "the story," from the officially sanctioned public school English of the mother country to American teenage slang to Rastafarian patois, show how lively a language can be and illustrate in many contexts the energy of metaphor in this vitality.

Naeman, Judith, and Carole G. Silver. 1983. *Kind Words*: A Thesaurus of Euphemisms. New York: Facts on File.

These authors define euphemizing as "substituting an unoffensive or pleasant term for a more explicit, offensive one, thereby veneering the truth by using kind words." Among the categories are Parts of the Body: Forbidden Territory; Parts of the Body: Neutral Territory; Blood, Sweat and Tears: Secretions, Excretions and Bathrooms; Death; Crime and Punishment; Sex; and The Language of Government and Game of War. This book should be previewed by teachers and may not be appropriate for young readers.

Partridge, Eric. 1966. *Origins: A Short Etymological Dictionary of Modern English*. New York: Macmillan.

The etymological histories of over 12,000 words are given in an especially readable style for this type of book. It is a manageable alternative to the *Oxford English Dictionary*.

————. 1974. *The Macmillan Dictionary of Historical Slang*. Abridged by Jacqueline Simpson. New York: Macmillan.

This abridgement of the original work, published in 1961, contains some 50,000 words and expressions already in use before World War I and going back to the seventeenth century. In addition to time of origin and etymology, the words are used in quotations and set in the contexts in which they first appeared.

Radford, Edwin. 1973. *To Coin a Phrase*: *A Dictionary of Origins*. London: Hutchinson.

This book reveals the metaphorical roots of many of our common expressions. The author exhumed many forgotten stories, apocryphal or otherwise, to provide a rich historical perspective on the language. Most readers will be enlightened to learn the sources of many of our dead metaphors, euphemisms, jargon, and idioms.

Rheingold, Howard. 1988. *They Have a Word for It*: *A Lighthearted Lexicon of Untranslatable Words and Phrases*. Los Angeles: J. P. Tarcher.

Since English has always been remarkably receptive to words and expressions from other languages—and with them the thoughts and perspectives of other cultures—why not a dictionary that deliberately sets as its task to introduce foreign terms and concepts for our use? Whether or not you believe that this book can help intercultural understanding and mind expansion, you will find its array of "untranslatable" words fascinating and suggestive for coining new terms in English.

Rogers, James. 1985. *The Dictionary of Clichés*. New York: Facts on File.

For readers who have heard or said such expressions as "that fits to a T," or "that's a dark horse," or "the bigger they come, the harder they fall," this is the chance to find out the events that generated our most enduring clichés.

Safire, William. 1988. *You Could Look It Up: More on Language*. New York: Random House.

This companion to *I Stand Corrected: More on Language* (1984) continues Safire's commentaries on word use and misuse. Many essays refer to metaphorical language, such as those detailing the etymologies of *huggermugger* and *Simon pure*. There are also essays on political rhetoric and doublespeak. Both volumes have extensive indexes that will facilitate the use of this resource for various purposes.

Thomas, Owen. 1969. *Metaphor and Related Subjects*. Edited by Richard Ohmann. New York: Random House.

One of the classic works on metaphor, written in the context of the restructuring of modern linguistics, Thomas's book contains a general introduction and a broad overview of figurative language. As he argues for greater awareness of the metaphorical basis of much thought, his intention is to help teachers and students become more precise and selective in their responses to, and uses of, metaphor.

Tuleja, Tad. 1989. *Foreignisms: A Dictionary of Foreign Expressions Commonly (And Not So Commonly) Used in English*. New York: Macmillan.

Tuleja has collected hundreds of foreign phrases and words assimilated into English without being Anglicized, such as *cordon bleu* (French for "blue ribbon"), *dogda rak svisnet* (Russian for "when the crayfish whistles," i.e., never), and *Schnapsidee* (German for a "crazy idea," or an idea coming from the liquor schnapps).

Urdang, Laurence, Nancy LaRoche, and Walter Hunsinger, eds. 1985. *Picturesque Expressions: A Thematic Dictionary*. Detroit: Gale Research.

Over 7,000 expressions are discussed in 408 thematic categories ranging from Abandonment to Zealousness. This collection provides the meanings and origins of such expressions as "the law of the jungle," "one for the Gipper," and "money doesn't grow on trees." The reader will learn that "mad money" once meant money a woman carried with her in case a date made advances. She could leave the scoundrel and pay her own cab fare home.

Williams, Raymond. 1976. *Keywords: A Vocabulary of Culture and Society*. New York: Oxford University Press.

The author has identified what he calls the "keywords" of the English language, those that presumably embody social and political attitudes, such as *alienation, equality, nature,* and *society*. He has written an essay on each, discussing both the gradual changes in meanings over time and the changes in thinking that these changes reflect. By examining the interactions of words, concepts, and experiences, he purports to be documenting the language of cultural transformation.

Winner, Ellen. 1988. *The Point of Words: Children's Understanding of Metaphor and Irony*. Cambridge, Mass.: Harvard University Press.

Winner provides the preschool and elementary school perspective on metaphor, which can be enlightening to middle school and high school teachers as well. She explores how children come to understand metaphor and irony. Examining research by many scholars in the field, she seeks to explain how knowledge of metaphors and the ability to use them evolve.

References

Documents indexed in *Resources in Education (RIE)* are denoted by a six-digit ED (ERIC Document) number. The majority of ERIC documents are reproduced on microfiche and may be viewed at ERIC collections in libraries and other institutions or can be ordered from the ERIC Document Reproduction Service (EDRS) in either paper copy or microfiche. For ordering information and price schedules, write or call EDRS, 7420 Fullerton Road, Suite 110, Springfield, VA 22153-2852. Phone: 1-800-443-ERIC or 703-440-1400. Fax: 703-440-1408.

Adler, Mortimer J., and Charles Van Doren. 1972. *How to Read a Book*. Rev. ed. New York: Simon and Schuster.

Adler, Renata. 1983. *Pitch Dark*. New York: Alfred A. Knopf.

Allen, Michele, and Lynn Burlbaw. 1987. "Making Meaning with a Metaphor." *Social Education* 51 (February): 142–43.

Anderson, Philip M. 1986. "Language Development and Aesthetic Modes of Thought." Paper presented at the annual meeting of the National Council of Teachers of English, San Antonio, Texas, 16–21 November.

Anderson, Philip M., and Bonnie S. Sunstein. 1987. "Teaching the Use of Metaphor in Science Writing." Paper presented at the annual meeting of the Conference on College Composition and Communication, Atlanta.

Andrews, Carol, ed. 1985. *The Ancient Egyptian Book of the Dead*. Translated by Raymond O. Faulkner. New York: Macmillan.

Bain, Carl E., et al. 1981. *The Norton Introduction to Literature*. New York: W. W. Norton.

Barrell, John, and Wendy Oxman. 1984. "Hi Heels and Walking Shadows: Metaphoric Thinking in Schools." Paper presented at the annual meeting of the American Educational Research Association, New Orleans. ED 245 056.

Bartel, Roland. 1983. *Metaphors and Symbols: Forays into Language*. Urbana, Ill.: National Council of Teachers of English.

Bartlett, John. 1980. *Bartlett's Famous Quotations*. Boston: Little, Brown.

———. 1986. *Bartlett's Familiar Quotations*. Edited by Emily Morison Beck. Boston: Little, Brown.

Berry, Ralph. 1978. *The Shakespearean Metaphor: Studies in Language and Form*. Totowa, N.J.: Rowman and Littlefield.

Berry, Wendell. 1988. "People, Land and Community." In *Multicultural Literacy*, edited by Rick Simonson and Scott Walker, 41–62. St. Paul: Graywolf Press.

Best, Judith. 1984. "Teaching Political Theory: Meaning through Metaphor." *Improving College and University Teaching* 32 (4): 165–68.

"Block That Metaphor." 1990. *The New Yorker,* 8 January, p. 100.

Blount, Roy, Jr. 1989. "No Sense Lending My Body an Ear." *Atlantic* (January): 34–35.

Brown, Richard Harvey. 1986. "Rhetoric and the Science of History: The Debate between Evolutionism and Empiricism as a Conflict of Metaphors." *Quarterly Journal of Speech* 72 (2): 148–61.

Bump, Jerome. 1985. "Metaphor, Creativity, and Technical Writing." *College Composition and Communication* 36 (4): 444–53.

Burke, William J. 1939. *The Literature of Slang.* New York: New York Public Library.

Burnett, David G. 1981. "Elementary Foreign Language Courses and General Education." *ADFL Bulletin* 12 (May): 9–13.

Burroway, Janet. 1987. *Writing Fiction: A Guide to Narrative Craft.* Boston: Little, Brown.

Callihan, E. L. 1969. *Grammar for Journalists.* Radnor, Penn.: Chilton.

Carpenter, Donna. 1988. "The Original *Fatal Attraction*: Metaphorical Thinking and *Medea.*" *English Journal* 77 (8): 42–44.

Carroll, Lewis [Charles Lutwidge Dodgson]. [1865] 1978. *Alice's Adventures in Wonderland.* In *Alice's Adventures in Wonderland and Through the Looking Glass.* London: Methuen Children's Books.

Cinnamond, Jeffrey. 1987. "Metaphors as Understanding: Recent Reform Reports on Education." Paper presented at the annual meeting of the Association for the Study of Higher Education, San Diego.

Connor, Kathleen, and Karen Johnson. 1985. "Perpetual Communication and Communicative Context in Metaphor Production." Paper presented at the annual convention of the American Psychological Association, Los Angeles, 23–27 August. ED 267 305.

Crooks, Robert L., and Jean Stein. 1988. *Psychology: Science, Behavior and Life.* New York: Holt, Rinehart and Winston.

Cullen, Countee. 1970. "From the Dark Tower." In *Black American Literature: Essays, Poetry, Fiction, Drama.* Edited by Darwin T. Turner. Columbus, Ohio: Charles E. Merrill.

Curtis, Helena, and N. Sue Barnes. 1985. *Invitation to Biology.* 4th ed. New York: Worth.

Daley, William. 1987. *The Chinese Americans.* New York: Chelsea House. (See pp. 71–73.)

Dawkins, Richard. 1989. "Put Your Money on Evolution." *New York Times Book Review,* 9 April, 35.

De Bono, Edward. 1976. *Teaching Thinking.* London: Maurice Temple Smith.

Delain, Marsha Taylor, P. David Pearson, and Richard C. Anderson. 1985. "Reading Comprehension and Creativity in Black Language Use: You Stand to

Gain by Playing the Sounding Game!" *American Educational Research Journal* 22 (2): 155–73.

Descartes, René. 1962. *Discourse on Method and Meditations.* Translated by John Veitch. LaSalle, Ill.: Open Court.

Dillard, Annie. 1989. *The Writing Life.* New York: Harper and Row.

Drewry, Henry N., et al. 1986. *United States History.* Vol. 1, *Beginning through Reconstruction.* Columbus, Ohio: Charles E. Merrill. (See pp. 294–95, 412, 468–69.)

Dufresne, Robert. 1991. "To Save a Life." In *The Way That Water Enters Stone.* New York: W. W. Norton.

Eckstein, Max A. 1983. "The Comparative Mind." *Comparative Education Review* 27 (3): 311–22.

Egan, Kieran. 1986. *Teaching as Storytelling: An Alternative Approach to Teaching and Curriculum in the Elementary School.* Chicago: University of Chicago Press.

Elbow, Peter. 1981. "Metaphors for Priming the Pump." In *Writing with Power: Techniques for Mastering the Writing Process.* New York: Oxford University Press. (See pp. 78–93.)

Eliade, Mircea. 1978. *From Primitives to Zen: A Thematic Sourcebook in the History of Religions.* New York: Harper and Row. (See pp. 139–44, 321–422.)

Elson, Martha. 1987. "Children and Death." *Louisville Courier-Journal,* 18 October, 21.

Espy, Willard R. 1981. *Have a Word on Me: A Celebration of Language.* New York: Simon and Schuster.

Feasley, Florence G. 1983. "Television Commercials: Symbols, Myths and Metaphors." Paper presented at the annual meeting of the Association for Education in Journalism and Mass Communications, Corvallis, Oregon.

Fleischmann, Glen H. 1971. *The Cherokee Removal, 1838: An Entire Indian Nation Is Forced Out of Its Homeland.* New York: Franklin Watts.

Flesch, Rudolph. 1957. *The Book of Unusual Quotations.* New York: Harper.

Floden, Robert E. 1986. *Explaining Learning: Biological and Cybernetic Metaphors.* Occasional Paper no. 99. East Lansing, Mich.: Institute for Research on Teaching, Michigan State University.

Fogelin, Robert J. 1988. *Figuratively Speaking.* New Haven, Conn.: Yale University Press.

Funk, Charles Earle. 1955. *Heavens to Betsy! And Other Curious Sayings.* New York: Harper.

Gannon, William J. 1984. "The Formulated Fix: The Role of Reification in the Diagnostic Process." *Psychology: A Quarterly Journal of Human Behavior* 21 (3/4): 43–48.

Gardner, Howard, and D. N. Perkins. 1990. "A Question of Creativity." *Harvard Alumni Gazette* (February): 15–16.

Geiger, William A., Jr. 1981. "Strengthening Language Control through Metaphor Analysis." Paper presented at the annual meeting of the Wyoming Conference on Freshman and Sophomore English, Laramie, 6–10 July. ED 251 851.

Geller, Linda Gibson. 1984. "Exploring Metaphor in Language Development and Learning." *Language Arts* 61 (2): 151–61.

Gibbs, Raymond W., Jr., and Annette Nagaoka. 1985. "Getting the Hang of American Slang: Studies on Understanding and Remembering Slang Metaphors." *Language and Speech* 28 (2): 177–94.

Gilgun, John. 1981. *Everything That Has Been Shall Be Again: The Reincarnation Fables*. Los Angeles: Bieler Press.

Greene, Graham. 1980. *Ways of Escape*. New York: Washington Square Press.

Gregory, Marshall. 1987. "If Education Is a Feast, Why Do We Restrict the Menu? A Critique of Pedagogical Metaphors." *College Teaching* 35 (3): 101–6.

Gyi, M. 1984. "Semantics of Nuclear Politics." *Et cetera: A Review of General Semantics* 41 (Summer): 135–47.

Hamlett, Ralph. 1987. "The Rhetorical Icon: Toward an Iconological Theory of U.S. Foreign Policy." Paper presented at the annual meeting of the Speech Communications Association, Boston.

Hannabus, Stuart. 1987. "Metaphors, Morality and Children's Books." *Use-of-English* 38 (3): 51–58.

Hausman, Carl R. 1989. *Metaphor and Art: Interactionism and Reference in the Verbal and Nonverbal Arts*. Cambridge, U.K.: Cambridge University Press.

Hawking, Stephen W. 1988. *A Brief History of Time: From the Big Bang to Black Holes*. New York: Bantam.

Herron, Carol. 1982. "Foreign-Language Learning Approaches as Metaphor." *Modern Language Journal* 66 (Autumn): 235–42.

Hirsch, E. D., Jr. 1989. "The Primal Scene of Education." *New York Review of Books* 36 (3; 2 March): 29–35.

al-Hoad, Abdul Latif. 1987. *Religions of the World: Folklore and Symbols*. New York: Bookwright Press. (See p. 21.)

Hoffman, Robert R. 1980. "Metaphor and Science." In *Cognition and Figurative Language*, edited by R. Honeck and R. Hoffman. Hillsdale, N.J.: Lawrence Erlbaum.

Hopkins, Thomas J. 1971. *The Hindu Religious Tradition*. Encino, Calif.: Dickenson Publishing Company.

Howard, Philip. 1988. *Winged Words*. New York: Oxford University Press.

Huff, Roland, and Charles R. Kline, Jr. 1987. *The Contemporary Writing Curriculum: Rehearsing, Composing, and Valuing*. New York: Teachers College Press.

Hughes, Langston. 1986. *The Dream Keeper and Other Poems*. New York: Alfred A. Knopf.

Ivie, Robert L. 1983. "Speaking 'Common Sense' about the Soviet Threat: Reagan's Rhetorical Stance." Paper presented at the annual meeting of the Western Speech Communication Association, Albuquerque, N.M.

Jobes, Gertrude. 1962. *Dictionary of Mythology, Folklore and Symbols.* New York: Scarecrow Press, Inc. (See pp. 420–22.)

Kidder, Rushworth M. 1988. "On Computer-Mindedness." *Christian Science Monitor,* 12 September.

Kilpatrick, James. 1990. "Writers Can Hit Home Runs, But They Also Swing and Miss." Bloomington, Ind., *Herald Times,* 25 February, p. A11, col. 4.

Kohl, Herbert. 1989. Reply to E. D. Hirsch's "The Primal Scene of Education." *New York Review of Books* 36 (6; 13 April): 50.

Lakoff, George. 1991. "Metaphors and War." Article published by computer network, Berkeley, Calif., 4 January.

Lakoff, George, and Mark Johnson. 1980. *Metaphors We Live By.* Chicago: University of Chicago Press.

Leacroft, Helen, and Richard Leacroft. 1963. *The Buildings of Ancient Egypt.* New York: W. R. Scott.

Leatherdale, W. H. 1974. *The Role of Analogy, Model and Metaphor in Science.* Amsterdam: North-Holland Publishing Company.

Lederer, Richard. 1987. *Anguished English: An Anthology of Accidental Assaults upon Our Language.* Charleston, S.C.: Wyrick.

———. 1989. *Crazy English: The Ultimate Joy Ride through Our Language.* New York: Pocket Books.

Littell, Joseph Fletcher, ed. 1972. *Coping with the Mass Media.* Evanston, Ill.: McDougal, Littell.

Low, Graham D. 1988. "On Teaching Metaphors." *Applied Linguistics* 9 (2): 125–47.

Lowrey, Burling, ed. 1960. *Twentieth Century Parody: American and British.* New York: Harcourt, Brace and World.

Luria, S. E. 1985. *A Slot Machine, a Broken Test Tube: An Autobiography.* New York: Harper and Row.

Lutz, William. 1989. *Doublespeak: From "Revenue Enhancement" to "Terminal Living": How Government, Business Advertisers and Others Use Language to Deceive You.* New York: Harper and Row.

MacCormac, Earl R. 1986. "Creative Metaphors." *Metaphor and Symbolic Activity* 1 (3): 171–84.

Mahood, Wayne. 1984. "Using Metaphors to Teach Social Studies." *Social Science Record* 21 (2) 12–14.

Mallon, Thomas. 1984. *A Book of One's Own: People and Their Diaries.* New York: Ticknor and Fields.

Martinelli, Kenneth J. 1987. "Thinking Straight about Thinking." *The School Administrator* 44 (1): 21–23.

Marzano, Robert, et al. 1988. *Dimensions of Thinking: A Framework for Curriculum and Instruction*. Arlington, Va.: Association for Supervision and Curriculum Development.

McBride, Mary, and Thomas Mullen. 1984. "Looking for Our Little Brother." *Et cetera: A Review of General Semantics* 41 (Summer): 148–51.

McEwan, Todd. 1984. "They Tell Me You Are Big." *Granta 10: Travel Writing*. Cambridge, U.K.: Granta Publications. (See pp. 13–15.)

McLeod, Irene Rutherford. 1957. "Lone Dog." In *Favorite Poems Old and New*. Edited by Helen Faris. New York: Doubleday.

McLuhan, Marshall. 1968. *War and Peace in the Global Village*. New York: McGraw-Hill.

McLuhan, Marshall, and Quentin Fiore. 1967. *The Medium Is the Massage*. New York: Bantam.

Miller, Hildy. 1987. "Teaching Everyday Metaphor." *Exercise Exchange* 33 (1): 11–13.

Miller, Jonathan. 1978. *The Body in Question*. New York: Random House.

Moore, Lorrie. 1990. *Like Life*. New York: Alfred A. Knopf.

Moore, Marianne. 1982. *The Complete Poems of Marianne Moore*. New York: Macmillan/Penguin Books.

Mosenthal, Peter B. 1987. "Metaphors for Reading in an Information Age." *The Reading Teacher* 41 (1): 82–84.

Munby, Hugh. 1986. "Metaphor in the Thinking of Teachers: An Exploratory Study." *Journal of Curriculum Studies* 18 (2): 197–209.

Muscari, Paul G. 1988. "The Metaphor in Science and in the Science Classroom." *Science Education* 72 (4): 423–31.

Nilsen, Don L. F. 1984. "Live, Dead, and Terminally Ill Metaphors in Computer Terminology; or, Who Is More Human, the Programmer or the Computer?" *Educational Technology* 24 (2): 27–29.

Orwell, George. 1946. *Critical Essays*. London: Secker and Warburg.

Owen, William Foster. 1984. "Toward a Sensory Education: Sensation as Metaphor." *Education* 105 (1): 79–81.

Ozick, Cynthia. 1986. "The Moral Necessity of Metaphor." *Harper's Magazine* 272 (1632): 62–68.

Palmatier, Robert A., and Harold L. Ray. 1989. *Sports Talk: A Dictionary of Sports Metaphors*. New York: Greenwood Press.

Partridge, Eric. 1959. *Origins: A Short Etymological Dictionary of Modern English*. New York: Macmillan.

Paul, Richard W. 1985. "Dialectical Reasoning." In *Developing Minds: A Resource Book for Teaching Thinking*, edited by Arthur L. Costa. Arlington, Va.: Association for Supervision and Curriculum Development.

Peele, Howard A. 1984. "Computer Metaphors: Approaches to Computer Literacy for Educators." Paper presented at the International Council for Computers in Education, Eugene, Ore. ED 240 704.

Perkins, D. N. 1981. *The Mind's Best Work*. Cambridge, Mass.: Harvard University Press.

Peterson, Linda. 1985. "Repetition and Metaphor in the Early Stages of Composing." *College Composition and Communication* 36 (4): 429–38.

Peterson, Willard J. 1988. "Squares and Circles: Mapping the History of Chinese Thought." *Journal of the History of Ideas* 49 (1): 47–60.

Prest, Peter, and Julie Prest. 1988. "Theory into Practice: Clarifying Our Intentions: Some Thoughts on the Application of Rosenblatt's Transactional Theory of Reading in the Classroom." *English Quarterly* 21 (2): 127–33.

Prestwood, Edward. 1984. *The Creative Writer's Phrase-Finder*. Palm Springs, Calif.: ETC Publications.

Pugh, Wesley. 1987. "Ethnography and School Improvement Research: Analyzing Metaphoric Language in the Interpretation of Instructional Leadership." Paper presented at the Annual Forum on Ethnography in Education Research, Philadelphia.

Quammen, David. 1988. *Blood Line: Stories of Fathers and Sons*. St. Paul: Graywolf Press.

Quinn, Arthur. 1982. *Figures of Speech: 60 Ways to Turn a Phrase*. Salt Lake City: G. M. Smith, Inc.

Radford, Edwin. 1973. *To Coin a Phrase: A Dictionary of Origins*. Edited and revised by Alan Smith. London: Hutchinson.

Rheingold, Howard. 1988. *They Have a Word for It: A Lighthearted Lexicon of Untranslatable Words and Phrases*. Los Angeles: J. P. Tarcher.

Ricoeur, Paul. 1977. *The Rule of Metaphor: Multi-Disciplinary Studies of the Creation of Meaning in Language*. Toronto: University of Toronto Press.

Room, Adrian. 1986. *Dictionary of Changes in Meaning*. London and New York: Routledge and Kegan Paul.

Rosenblatt, Louise M. 1938. *Literature as Exploration*. New York: D. Appleton-Century.

———. 1978. *The Reader, the Text, the Poem: The Transactional Theory of the Literary Work*. Carbondale, Ill.: Southern Illinois University Press.

Rosenthal, Andrew. 1990. "Bush Vows Not to Be Cowed by the Taking of 'Hostages'; Iraq Shifts Them to Targets." *New York Times*, 21 August, A1, A7.

Rubin, John. 1988. "Anatomy of Analogy." *Psychology Today* 22 (2): 12.

Sacks, Oliver W. 1990. *The Man Who Mistook His Wife for a Hat: And Other Clinical Tales*. New York: Harper and Row.

Sanders, Donald, and Judith Sanders. 1987. "Capturing the Magic of Metaphor." *Learning* (February): 37–39.

Sapir, Edward. 1956. Quoted in *Language, Thought and Reality* by Benjamin Whorf. Cambridge, Mass.: MIT Press.

Schiappa, Edward. 1987. "The Rhetoric of Nukespeak." EDRS report. ED 286 302.

Schulz, Bruno. 1979. *Sanatorium under the Sign of the Hourglass*. Trans. by Celina Wieniewska. New York: Viking Penguin. Originally published in Polish as *Sanatorium pod Klepsydra*, 1937.

Shapiro, Stephanie. 1988. "Changing Metaphors Can Help the World, Scholar Says." *The Indianapolis Star*, 25 November.

Sheldon, William H. (with C. Wesley Dupertuis and Eugene McDermott). 1954. *Atlas of Men: A Guide for Somatotyping the Adult Male at All Ages*. New York: Gramercy.

Silko, Leslie M. 1986. *Ceremony*. New York: Viking Penguin.

Siltanen, Susan A. 1986. " 'Butterflies or Rainbows': A Developmental Investigation of Metaphor Comprehension." *Communication Education* 35 (1): 1–11.

Simpson, James B. 1988. *Simpson's Contemporary Quotations*. Boston: Houghton Mifflin.

Simpson, Mona. 1988. *Anywhere but Here*. New York: Vintage Books.

Smith, Lee. 1990. *Me and My Baby View the Eclipse: Stories*. New York: Putnam Publishing Group.

Smith, Leonora H. 1988. "Revising the Real Way: Metaphors for Selecting Detail." *English Journal* 77 (8): 38–41.

Solomon, Jack. 1988. *The Signs of Our Time: Semiotics, the Hidden Messages of Environments, Objects, and Cultural Images*. Los Angeles: J. P. Tarcher.

Spring, Joel. 1989. *Conflict of Interests: The Politics of American Education*. New York: Longman. (See pp. 27, 56–57.)

Stambovsky, Phillip. 1988. "Metaphor and Historical Understanding." *History and Theory: Studies in the Philosophy of History* 27 (2): 125–34.

Stevens, Wallace. 1982. *Collected Poems*. New York: Vintage Books.

Sting [Gordon Sumner]. 1987. Notes to "Lazarus Heart" on the record album *Nothing like the Sun*. Los Angeles: A&M Records.

Thomas, Lewis. 1974. *The Lives of a Cell: Notes of a Biology Watcher*. New York: Viking Penguin.

Thomas, Owen. 1969. *Metaphor and Related Subjects*. New York: Random House.

Thompson, Timothy N. 1986. "Analoguing Creativity and Culture: A Method for Metaphors." Portsmouth, N.H.: Heinemann. ED 282 263.

Thoreau, Henry David. [1854] 1948. *Walden; or, Life in the Woods*. New York: Holt, Rinehart and Winston.

Ting-Toomey, Stella. 1983. "The World Hypothesis: Implications for Innercultural Communication Research." Paper presented at the annual meeting of the International Communication Association, Dallas, May.

Todes, Daniel P. 1987. "Darwin's Malthusian Metaphor and Russian Evolutionary Thought, 1859–1917." *Isis* 78 (December): 537–51.

Tomlinson, Barbara. 1986. "Cooking, Mining, Gardening, Hunting: Metaphorical Stories Writers Tell about Their Composing Processes." *Metaphor and Symbolic Activity* 1 (1): 57–79.

———. 1988. "Tuning, Tying, and Training Texts: Metaphors for Revision." *Written Communication* 5 (1): 58–81.

Turkle, Sherry. 1984. *The Second Self: Computers and the Human Spirit*. New York: Simon and Schuster.

Turner, Mark. 1987. *Death Is the Mother of Beauty: Mind, Metaphor, Criticism*. Chicago: University of Chicago Press.

"Unfinished Revolution." 1990. *Time*. 8 January, 30.

Ventura, Michael. 1988. "Report from El Dorado." In *Multicultural Literacy: The Opening of the American Mind*, edited by R. Simonsen and S. Walker. St. Paul: Graywolf Press.

Vosniadou, Stella. 1986. *Children and Metaphors*. Technical Report no. 370. Center for the Study of Reading, University of Illinois at Urbana-Champaign. Cambridge, Mass.: Bolt, Beranek and Newman. ED 267 378.

Vygotsky, L. S. 1978. *Mind in Society: The Development of Higher Psychological Processes*. Cambridge: Harvard University Press.

Walker, Alice. 1988. "What's Hair Got to Do with It? Oppressed Hair Puts a Ceiling on the Brain." *MS* 16 (12, June): 52–53.

Wambi, Bruno. 1988. "A Carnivore Called Science." *Third World* no. 14 (May/June): 53.

Waters, Margaret. 1984. "Metaphor in the Lives of Children." Paper presented at the annual meeting of the New York State English Council, Amherst, N.Y.

Wheelwright, Philip E. 1962. *Metaphor and Reality*. Bloomington, Ind.: Indiana University Press.

White, T. H. 1954. *The Book of Beasts: Being a Translation from a Latin Bestiary of the Twelfth Century*. London: Cape.

Whorf, Benjamin. 1956. *Language, Thought and Reality: Selected Writings of Benjamin Lee Whorf*. Cambridge, Mass.: MIT Press.

Williams, Linda V. 1983. *Teaching for the Two-Sided Mind: A Guide to Right-Brain–Left-Brain Education*. Englewood Cliffs, N.J.: Prentice-Hall.

Wing, R. L. 1979. *The I Ching Workbook*. Garden City, N.Y.: Doubleday.

Winner, Ellen. 1988. *The Point of Words: Children's Understanding of Metaphor and Irony*. Cambridge, Mass.: Harvard University Press.

Wolfe, Tom. 1987. *Bonfire of the Vanities*. New York: Farrar, Straus and Giroux.

Woods, Geraldine. 1989. *Affirmative Action*. New York: Franklin Watts.

Yaukey, John. 1990. "The Search for Gravity." *Louisville Courier-Journal*, 18 April.

Authors

Sharon L. Pugh is associate professor of Language Education and director of the Learning Skills Center at Indiana University. She was director of the Young Authors Program in the Indianapolis Public Schools and has published short fiction in several literary magazines. She also teaches and does research in the areas of critical reading and uses of multicultural tradebooks in language arts teaching.

Jean Wolph Hicks has worked with preservice teachers at the University of Louisville School of Education since 1987. In 1991 she received the Education Student Council's Outstanding Undergraduate Teacher Award. Previously she taught language arts and journalism at the middle and high school levels in Oldham and Jefferson counties, Kentucky.

Marcia Davis is currently doing graduate work in Language Education at Indiana University. Before joining Sharon Pugh's metaphor team, she found joy as a middle school English teacher. She also coached students in Olympics of the Mind, a program for imaginative thinking. Her professional writing includes short stories and literature reviews as well as editing.

Tonya Venstra is a graduate student in Language Education at Indiana University with a special interest in adult and community literacy. As the supervisor of the Indiana University Reading Practicum Center, she develops and implements programs for reluctant readers. She has also been involved in home schooling.